3D Environment [
Blender

Enhance your modeling, texturing, and lighting skills to create realistic 3D scenes

Abdelilah Hamdani

BIRMINGHAM—MUMBAI

3D Environment Design with Blender

Group Product Manager: Rohit Rajkumar
Publishing Product Manager: Vaideeshwari MuraliKrishnan
Senior Editor: Mark D'Souza
Senior Content Development Editor: Feza Shaikh
Technical Editor: Simran Ali
Copy Editor: Safi s Editing
Project Coordinator: Sonam Pandey
Proofreader: Safi s Editing
Indexer: Manju Arasan
Production Designer: Alishon Mendonca
Marketing Coordinator: Nivedita Pandey

First published: January 2023
Production reference: 1200123

Published by Packt Publishing Ltd.
Livery Place
35 Livery Street
Birmingham
B3 2PB, UK.

ISBN 978-1-80323-585-1

www.packtpub.com

To my awesome mom and dad, for giving me the advantage and opportunity to succeed. To my two best mentors, MJ Demarco and Jim Rohn, who opened my eyes, guided me, and are still guiding me throughout my entrepreneurial journey.

– Abdelilah Hamdani

Foreword

In 2019, I found a course called *Learn to Create Photorealistic Exterior Environments* by Abdelilah Hamdani. That was one of the courses that changed my life. Back then, I didn't know much about Blender and from that course, I learned what was needed to create a good-looking photorealistic scene.

With *3D Environment Design with Blender*, you will have a better experience than I had in 2019 because this book will take your learning process even further, showing step by step what you need to do to make your scene realistic. For example, matching a Blender scene to a real-world scale and how to make a photorealistic material. Those subjects are easily overlooked by beginners and even more advanced 3D artists, making it difficult to realize why your scene doesn't look good.

You will also take a dive into how to create UV mapping and nature assets (plants, flowers, and rocks) and how to scatter them; landscapes, realistic rivers, procedural good-looking materials and how to apply them; photorealistic lighting and rendering; and finally, compositing. In summary, everything you need to create a complete and beautiful realistic scene.

Everything is explained in detail and whenever possible, examples from daily life are given to make it even easier to understand some concepts.

Reading *3D Environment Design with Blender*, you will have a complete journey from start to finish, very well explained. You won't get confused because the chapters have a connection, meaning everything makes sense. You will just need to follow it through to the end and you will come out a better artist.

I can say that my first contact with Abdelilah Hamdani's course back in 2019 changed my life because today I make a living with Blender products – something I didn't think would be possible. This book could be your first step too, to help you start making a living with Blender.

Carlos Barreto

Creator of CEB Studio

Contributors

About the author

Abdelilah Hamdani is a photorealistic environment designer and 3D animator who is experienced in producing 3D art in a professional environment. Projects he has worked on include the 2020 Kuwait election and the US Gambian bridge construction. Abdelilah is also an online instructor who has taught more than 25,000 students worldwide. He is the founder of Reality Fakers, a platform that teaches 3D photorealism.

About the reviewer

Jarosław Dzedzej is an experienced 3D artist who has been using Blender since 2008. After graduating from the Academy of Fine Arts in Gdańsk, Poland, with a Master of Arts title in interior design, he started using Blender as his main tool to visualize his own projects as well as commercial archviz commissions. Diving deep into 3D art, this area of creativity became his main focus and passion. He also shares his knowledge with the 3D community through video tutorials on the GarageFarm.NET Academy channel on YouTube. He loves drawing with ink and digital painting. He shares a lot of his creations on his social media (YouTube, Twitter, Instagram, and Mastodon).

Table of Contents

3

Efficient Unwrapping and Texturing in Blender   45

4

Creating Realistic Natural Plants in Blender   65

5

Achieve Photorealistic Lighting in Your Environment
with Blender   93

Part 2: Creating Realistic Landscapes in Blender

6

Creating Realistic Landscapes in Blender   121

7

Creating and Animating Realistic, Natural-Looking Water   145

8

Creating Procedural Mud Material   165

9

Texturing the Landscape with Mud Material   193

Part 3: Creating Natural Assets

10

Creating Natural Assets: Rock   217

11

Creating Realistic Flowers in Blender   241

Part 4: Rendering Epic Landscape Shots

12

13

Preface

Creating 3D environments is now more popular than ever. It's a skill that every 3D designer should master. Whether you are or want to be a freelancer, or you're simply a hobbyist, this book will serve you well.

This book will give you a great insight into how 3D works, starting by showing you the mistakes most 3D designers make that prevent people from achieving great results. I have taught more than 25,000 students and responded to hundreds of students' questions. Trust me – I've seen it all. To give you the maximum value, there is no better way to start this book than to show you these mistakes and how you can avoid them. Then, in later chapters, we will dive into the creation of an epic landscape environment.

This book will give you enough knowledge and inspiration to create multiple environments, fill your portfolio, and attract clients and companies.

What makes this book special is that it's sequential – each chapter moves you forward and contributes to the final result. We will only learn the things we need and anything you will learn, you will apply.

Each chapter will upgrade your skills and push you forward toward achieving the final result, which is the creation of realistic landscape environments in Blender.

Who this book is for

This book is for advanced 3D designers who are eager to learn and upgrade their 3D design skills; hobbyists of Blender who want to fast-track their understanding of 3D environment design; and freelancers who want to upgrade their 3D skills, fill their portfolios, and attract clients and companies that require 3D design work.

What this book covers

Chapter 1, Most Common Modeling Mistakes That Prevent You from Achieving Photorealism, will cover all the mistakes that designers make in 3D modeling and scale matching and will show the reader the ways to fix and overcome these challenges by working on a real wood cabin reference.

Chapter 2, The Basics of Realistic Texturing in Blender, will highlight the importance of using different texturing maps to achieve photorealism. We will learn how to create a real wood material from scratch using procedural texturing.

Chapter 3, Efficient Unwrapping and Texturing in Blender, will go through the process of unwrapping the wood cabin and texturing it in Blender – starting by importing materials from one scene into another, understanding how UV mapping works, and using the **Displace** modifier to add random details to the wood geometry.

Chapter 4, Creating Realistic Natural Plants in Blender, will involve creating a ground under our wood cabin, using the **Proportional Editing** tool to add nice hills to the ground. Then, we will go through the process of creating, unwrapping, and texturing different types of plants and leaves. Next, we will learn how to use the **Particle System** tool to scatter objects randomly across a surface, scattering plants and leaves all over the ground.

Chapter 5, Achieve Photorealistic Lighting in Your Environment with Blender, will detail three ways to lighten the wood cabin scene. We will achieve lighting that matches the same lighting we have in the wood cabin reference we're using.

Chapter 6, Creating Realistic Landscapes in Blender, will guide you on how to create realistic snow and rocky mountains. We will learn to install the **A.N.T** add-on, create various landscapes, tweak its settings and change its shape to make it look as realistic as possible.

Chapter 7, Creating and Animating Realistic, Natural-Looking Water, will handle the step of creating a realistic water shader. We will learn to mix between the **Glass BSDF** and **Transparency BSDF** nodes to create a nice reflective and refractive surface. Then we will learn to animate the waves on the surface of the water by inserting keyframes into the **Timeline** editor.

Chapter 8, Creating Procedural Mud Material, will tap into the unlimited potential of Blender's incredibly powerful node editor. You will learn to create a **Mud** material using procedural texturing by combining many different layers of details, such as adding water puddles, stones, and mud details.

Chapter 9, Texturing the Landscape with Mud Material, will entail texturing the landscape with the **Mud** material. You will learn how to mix different materials – here, the rocky snow and mud. You will also learn how to optimize and organize your node setup using groups.

Chapter 10, Creating Natural Assets: Rock, will teach you how to create realistic rock assets. These rocks are perfect for giving a realistic and natural feeling to our landscape environment.

Chapter 11, Creating Realistic Flowers in Blender, will describe how to create organic-looking flowers for our landscape environment based on real references.

Chapter 12, Using Particle System to Scatter Objects in Blender, will outline how to use the **Particle System** tool in Blender to scatter flowers and rocks throughout our landscape environment. You will understand **Particle System** in Blender, and how to add and place particles in a specific chosen area, as well as changing the scale and rotation of particles while controlling their number.

Chapter 13, Finalizing the Landscape Scene – Lighting, Rendering, and Compositing, will sum up our processes and the book by teaching you how to aim your camera to render awesome landscape shots. Next, you will learn some compositing tricks to make the final render stand out.

To get the most out of this book

Blender is free software.

Throughout this book, we'll be using some techniques that require you to have a decent setup. Anything above an i5 8gen, 16 GB RAM, and GTX 1060 will do the job.

Software/hardware covered in the book	Operating system requirements
Blender 3.3 or above	Windows, macOS, or Linux
fSpy	Windows

Have Blender 3.3 installed and let's dive in!

If you are using the digital version of this book, we advise you to type the code yourself or access the code from the book's GitHub repository (a link is available in the next section). Doing so will help you avoid any potential errors related to the copying and pasting of code.

Download the example code files

You can download the example code files for this book from GitHub at `https://github.com/PacktPublishing/3D-Environment-Design-with-Blender`. If there's an update to the code, it will be updated in the GitHub repository.

We also have other code bundles from our rich catalog of books and videos available at `https://github.com/PacktPublishing/`. Check them out!

Download the color images

We also provide a PDF file that has color images of the screenshots and diagrams used in this book.

You can download it here: `https://packt.link/KOKhm`.

Conventions used

There are a number of text conventions used throughout this book.

`Code in text`: Indicates code words in text, database table names, folder names, filenames, file extensions, pathnames, dummy URLs, user input, and Twitter handles. Here is an example: "Create a new material called `Mountain`."

Bold: Indicates a new term, an important word, or words that you see onscreen. For instance, words in menus or dialog boxes appear in bold. Here is an example: "Also, to see the effect more clearly, make sure to change the color of the **Base Color** map to black."

> **Tips or important notes**
> Appear like this.

Get in touch

Feedback from our readers is always welcome.

General feedback: If you have questions about any aspect of this book, email us at `customercare@ packtpub.com` and mention the book title in the subject of your message.

Errata: Although we have taken every care to ensure the accuracy of our content, mistakes do happen. If you have found a mistake in this book, we would be grateful if you would report this to us. Please visit `www.packtpub.com/support/errata` and fill in the form.

Piracy: If you come across any illegal copies of our works in any form on the internet, we would be grateful if you would provide us with the location address or website name. Please contact us at `copyright@packt.com` with a link to the material.

If you are interested in becoming an author: If there is a topic that you have expertise in and you are interested in either writing or contributing to a book, please visit `authors.packtpub.com`.

Share Your Thoughts

Once you've read, we'd love to hear your thoughts! Scan the QR code below to go straight to the Amazon review page for this book and share your feedback.

`https://packt.link/r/1803235853`

Your review is important to us and the tech community and will help us make sure we're delivering excellent quality content. Download a free PDF copy of this book

Download a free PDF copy of this book

Thanks for purchasing this book!

Do you like to read on the go but are unable to carry your print books everywhere?

Is your eBook purchase not compatible with the device of your choice?

Don't worry, now with every Packt book you get a DRM-free PDF version of that book at no cost.

Read anywhere, any place, on any device. Search, copy, and paste code from your favorite technical books directly into your application.

The perks don't stop there, you can get exclusive access to discounts, newsletters, and great free content in your inbox daily

Follow these simple steps to get the benefits:

1. Scan the QR code or visit the link below

https://packt.link/free-ebook/9781803235851

2. Submit your proof of purchase
3. That's it! We'll send your free PDF and other benefits to your email directly

Part 1:
Turn a Real Reference into a
Realistic 3D Scene in Blender

Before we can start creating our landscape project, there are some tricks and tools that you need to know about. First, it's best to know the most common modeling mistakes that prevent most 3D designers from achieving photorealism. Next, you will learn the basics of realistic texturing, good UV mapping, and lighting. Then we will put everything we've learned together to turn a real wood cabin reference into a realistic 3D scene in Blender.

This part includes the following chapters:

- *Chapter 1, Most Common Modeling Mistakes That Prevent You from Achieving Photorealism*
- *Chapter 2, The Basics of Realistic Texturing in Blender*
- *Chapter 3, Efficient Unwrapping and Texturing in Blender*
- *Chapter 4, Creating Realistic Natural Plants in Blender*
- *Chapter 5, Achieve Photorealistic Lighting in Your Environment with Blender*

1

Most Common Modeling Mistakes That Prevent You from Achieving Photorealism

Have you ever tried to create a photorealistic scene in **Blender**? Are you looking for a step-by-step formula to help you achieve **photorealism** in Blender? Do you find yourself stuck getting the right settings? If so, you're not alone.

In this chapter, we're going to break down the three modeling mistakes that most 3D designers make that prevent them from achieving photorealism in Blender.

Modeling represents the foundation for what's coming next: texturing, UV mapping, lighting, compositing, and rendering. Getting the foundation wrong will make all your efforts be in vain, so the goal of this chapter is to help you get the modeling foundation right.

The first mistake is relying on only your eyes to estimate the scale of objects you're modeling. When it comes to photorealism, getting the right scale plays a crucial role. So, we'll be discussing the Blender unit system and how to perform research to get the right, realistic measurements of objects before modeling them.

The second mistake is related to scale matching: most designers immediately dive into creating a 3D scene based on a real reference without doing any scale matching. This makes it really hard to get the same camera settings, such as position, rotation, and focal length, that an actual photographer would use. This results in an unmatched result to the reference you're working with. To overcome this issue, we will learn to use fSpy, a tool that allows you to replicate the camera settings adopted by a photographer (focal length, camera position, and rotation) when taking a picture of an actual image and export it into Blender. We will explore how the fSpy interface works, how to use it, and how to install the fSpy add-on into Blender and import fSpy project files.

The third mistake is modeling without the bevel modifier on. By the end of this chapter, you will understand the importance of using the **bevel modifier** when modeling and the role it plays in achieving photorealism. You will also understand the different beveling settings and how they work inside Blender.

In this chapter, we'll be covering the following topics:

- The importance of using a real-world scale
- Learning scale matching using the fSpy program
- The importance of using the bevel modifier when modeling

Technical requirements

This chapter requires a Mac or PC capable of running Blender Version 3.0 or above.

You can download the resources for this chapter from GitHub at `https://github.com/PacktPublishing/3D-Environment-Design-with-Blender/tree/main/chapter-1`

The importance of using a real-world scale

When creating complex scenes in Blender, it's easy to fall into the trap of eyeballing the scale of objects when modeling them, without taking the right measurements. This can lead to multiple problems that will prevent you later on from achieving a photorealistic and eye-pleasing result.

We think our eyes are accurate – *"I know how large this window is, it's this size"*; however, we're really bad at estimating measurements simply because we give more emphasis to the things that we pay attention to and neglect the parts we deem unimportant.

This then affects the photorealistic aspect of your scene: you end up wondering what is wrong with your scene. Something just looks off and you don't know what it is. You start messing around with the materials and the lighting, and maybe those are perfect but then you realize the foundation was wrong. So, it is important to get this modeling foundation right.

So, the solution is to *always use a real-world scale*.

Let's say you're designing a wood cabin; the first thing you need to do is research on Google: `What is the height of a log cabin?`.

3 meters

A log cabin with a pent or hip roof can have a total height of **up to 3 meters**, while a log cabin with an apex roof can have a total height of up to 4 meters. The log cabin must not have internal dimensions above 30m2 and must not be installed in front of the property.

https://www.tigersheds.com › page › log-cabin-planning-...   ⋮

Do I Need Planning Permission for my Log Cabin? - Tiger Sheds

 ❓ About featured snippets • 🔳 Feedback

Figure 1.1 – Google search for the height of a log cabin

So, now we understand that a wood cabin must not exceed 3 meters in height, so everything between 2 and 3 meters should be reasonable. With the apex roof included, another meter is added.

Since we must not exceed 30 m2, we can give a dimension of 5 m wide and 6 m long (5 m × 6 m = 30 m2.).

Next, we will check the Blender unit scale:

1. Go to **Scene Properties**.

2. Click on the **Units** tab.

3. Then choose the **Unit System** measurement that suits you.

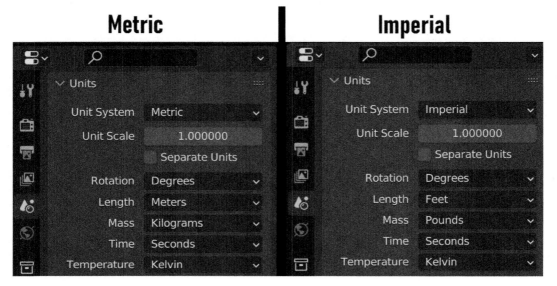

Figure 1.2 – Blender scene properties units system

Choosing **Metric** will measure the length in meters and mass in kilograms, unlike **Imperial**, which will measure the length in feet and mass in pounds. This is the right way to set real-world measurements in Blender.

Another good reason to always use a real-world scale is because of how physics simulation works in Blender. Physics in Blender, such as gravity, rigid body, and mass, relies on real measurements to work properly.

To emphasize this even more, let's create a sphere; by default, the sphere will be 2 meters in diameter. Next, we go to **Physics Properties**, and we click on **Rigid Body** while making sure the sphere is selected. Under the **Settings** tab, you'll see that **Mass** is set to **1 kg** by default. This means that the 2-meter diameter sphere you've just created has a weight of 1 kg.

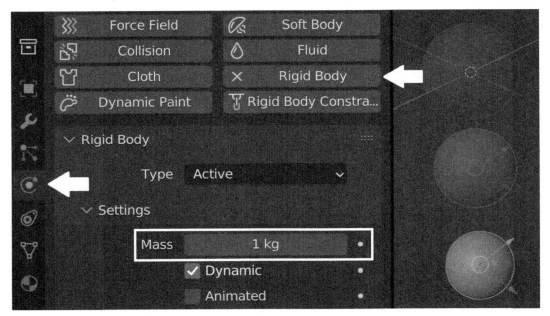

Figure 1.3 – Blender physics properties

Now, if you press the spacebar, the physics simulation will start. Our sphere will fall down due to gravitational force. If we change the scale of our sphere to something around 0.2 meters and give it a weight of 4.5 kg, our sphere will behave exactly like a bowling ball. Similarly, if we scale down our sphere diameter to 5 cm and a weight of 170 g, our ball will act like a billiard ball.

The bottom line is, always use a real-world scale: it's crucial for achieving photorealistic results that match reality.

Now that we have seen the importance of using real-scale measurements when modeling, let's learn scale matching. It's an awesome trick that allows us to get almost the exact camera settings from an image reference, so that we can then easily recreate the scene in Blender.

Learning scale matching using fSpy

Next, let's learn scale matching. To put things in perspective, let's say you have a real reference that you want to replicate as a 3D scene. You can load it as a camera background, and start modeling it, but soon enough, you will encounter a big challenge, which is to match the same position, rotation, and focal length of the camera that took the shot.

You can see in this example the difficulties in matching the same log cabin reference:

Figure 1.4 – Wood cabin model not matching the reference

Our objective is to place the modeled cube exactly on top of the cabin reference (the red lines must be on top of the green lines). The corners must match each other in order to have true camera matching; doing it by eye won't cut it, so we need to do it the right way.

Luckily, we have fSpy, which is a free open source software program that allows us to estimate the camera parameters from an image reference and import it into Blender.

The way it works is as follows: you import the reference image whose camera settings you want to match, and you choose the number of vanishing points; you will find this feature on the top left side panel of the fSpy program.

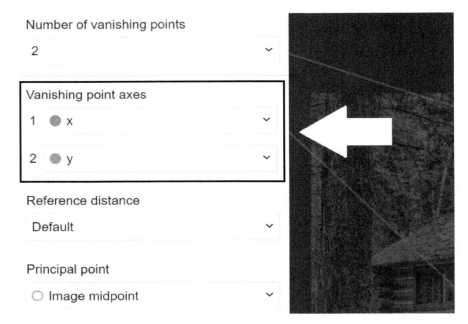

Figure 1.5 – Vanishing point axes in the fSpy interface

Basically, the number vanishing points depends on the type of reference you're using:

- **One vanishing point**: This means that your reference has a point where all lines meet. If you follow any parallel lines in the reference, they will end up meeting at one point.

Figure 1.6 – Example of one vanishing point reference

- **Two vanishing points**: You can use two vanishing points in case there are two kinds of parallel lines in your reference, with each side seemingly slowly fading away into distance; they will meet at a certain point in the distance. An example would be something like this:

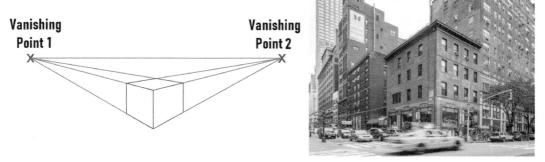

Figure 1.7 – Example of two vanishing points

The camera parameters are as follows: focal length, rotation, and position of the camera.

In our case, we will be using a wood cabin reference that has two vanishing points; you can tell this by following the wood lines on both the front and side faces of the cabin. You can download this image from GitHub at https://github.com/PacktPublishing/3D-Environment-Design-with-Blender/blob/main/Wood%20Cabin%20Reference.jpeg

Figure 1.8 – Wood cabin reference

Alright, now let's start using fSpy.

Downloading fSpy

First, let's download fSpy. You can google `fSpy` or use this official website link: `https://www.fspy.io`.

Once on the webpage, we will do the following:

1. Click the green **Download** button.

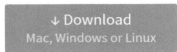

fSpy is open source software and **totally free to download and use**. But just in case you think it makes sense to pay for fSpy, here's a donate button! Pay as much or as little as you want.

Figure 1.9 – fSpy download button

You will be directed to GitHub.

2. Under **Assets**, we will be downloading the `fSpy-1.0.3-ia32-win.zip` file, which is 47.2MB Unzip it, and double click on the *fSpy* icon.

3. Inside the program interface, on the top bar, go to **File -> Open Image.**

4. Choose the image reference shown in *Figure 1.8.*

If done right, this is what you will get:

Figure 1.10 – Wood cabin reference loaded into fSpy

After downloading fSpy, put our image reference into it and set the x and z axes to match our reference lines. Now, it's time to understand the fSpy interface and how we can manipulate it to get the best results.

Breaking down the fSpy tools

Alright, let's get to work on using the fSPy tools:

1. Make sure you're using two vanishing points; you will find this feature on the top left side panel (see *Figure 1.5*).

2. Make the image reference clear, then on the left side, down below, uncheck the **Dim image** box.

3. On the left panel, switch the y axis to the z axis to get the vertical proportion of your reference.

4. Align the x and z axes with the most obvious lines in our reference.

In our case, we can rely on the wood lines and roof. Make sure the lines you choose are far away from each other; this will allow the fSpy to caliber the scene much better.

The final result should be as follows:

Figure 1.11 – fSpy vanishing point axes aligned with the reference lines

Sometimes the focal length generated by fSpy won't be accurate, so you have to tweak it a little bit manually – it's really easy to do so.

Adjusting the focal length

To adjust the focal length, perform the following steps:

1. On the left panel, change **Principal point** to **Manual**. By default, **Principal point** will be set to **Image midpoint**. As soon as you change it to **Manual**, a yellow point will appear in the middle of your reference.

2. If you grab it and move it a little bit, you will change the focal length of your camera. You will see that on the right panel under the **Field of view** tab, beside the **Horizontal** value:

Figure 1.12 – Changing the focal length settings in fSpy

Alright, now let's save this project: go to **File** then click on **Save As** and save the fSpy file to your desktop.

Exporting the fSpy file

Now, let's export this fSpy file into Blender. To do that, we must install an addon that allows us to do this.

The addon is available at this GitHub link for download: `https://github.com/PacktPublishing/3D-Environment-Design-with-Blender/blob/d71de483c88180ac12dc0e6738ce3a7425b00389/chapter-1/fSpy-Blender-Addon.zip`.

Once you download the `fSpy-Blender-Addon.zip` file, make sure to not unzip this file.

Once you get the addon zip file, we can now jump into Blender and install it. So, in our Blender interface, click on **Edit** -> **Preferences**, click on **Add-ons** on the middle left side, then on the top right, click on **Install** and choose the `fSpy-Blender-Addon.zip` file. Then you should see a message below saying that the module is installed. Also make sure that you enabled the fSpy addon box **Import-Export: Import fSpy project**.

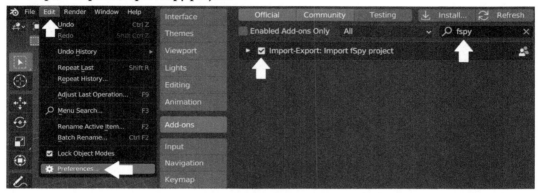

Figure 1.13 – Installing the fSpy add-on in Blender

Alright, now let's import the fSpy file we created with the fSpy program. If you follow the previous steps, when you go to **File** and **Import**, you will see that you have the possibility to import fSpy files into Blender. Just click on **Import** and choose the fSpy file we created earlier, then you will see the following:

Figure 1.14 – Importing the wood cabin fSpy file into Blender

This is the benefit of using fSpy; now we have camera settings that match those of our photographer who took this shot. The same camera focal length, camera position, and rotation has been replicated. From now on, we can go and start building our scene.

Building our scene

First, let's exit the camera view; you can do so by pressing the number *0* on the numpad.

Figure 1.15 – First three steps to creating the wood cabin scene

We begin by making a ground plane (**1**) and adding a simple cube (**2**), making sure it's on the top of the grid.

Place the cube on the corner of the cabin reference:

Figure 1.16 – Putting the modeled cube in the corner of the reference

Placing the cube on the corner of the cabin reference will allow you to get the right start. Otherwise, you will be stuck not knowing where to put the initial cube. Another note is to move the cube only along the x and y axes; we need to keep it on the floor.

Figure 1.17 – Four steps to model the wood cabin in Blender

Next, we can proceed and create the basic shape of the wood cabin that we have in our reference:

1. Select the cube and enter edit mode (press **Tab** to toggle between edit and object mode).
2. In edit mode, select the front face, and move it to cover the length of the cabin wood. Also, align the backface with the back of the wood cabin reference.
3. Select the top face and move it upward until it reaches the beginning of the roof.
4. Press E to extrude it more upward until it reaches the top of the reference.
5. You can scale it on the y axis to make that A shape.

As you can see, we will now have a perfect match to our reference image:

Figure 1.18 – The final result of the modeled wood cabin

Also, make sure that you are using the measurements we set earlier; to do so without distorting the camera angle, make sure that you scale everything up one at a time, the camera included.

Now that we have finished matching the same scale of our reference and made a *simple* wood cabin, you can see the beauty of scale matching; our camera settings in Blender now perfectly match the camera settings used to take the reference image. Both have the same focal length and rotation. This is an excellent start to achieving a photorealistic result.

Next, we will cover one of the most fatal mistakes that prevents most 3D designers from achieving photorealism: forgetting the bevel modifier.

The importance of using the bevel modifier when modeling

One of the fatal mistakes that most 3D designers commit that prevent them from achieving photorealistic results is modeling without using the bevel modifier. Let's see a quick example in Blender to emphasize this theory.

> **Bevel modifier**
>
> The bevel modifier gives you the ability to bevel the edges of the mesh it is applied to. Basically, it adds edge lines in between the mesh corners (see *Figure 1.17*). It might seem like a simple step, but the effect the bevel modifier has is enormous for achieving photorealism; we'll see that later.

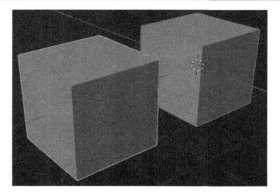

Figure 1.19 – Creation of two cubes

For our example, let's use two cubes, one with the bevel modifier applied to it (red cube) and another without any beveling (blue cube). To apply beveling to the red cube, let's perform the following steps:

1. Go to **Modifier Properties** (wrench icon), select **Add Modifier**, and choose the **Bevel** modifier:

Figure 1.20 – Bevel modifier settings in Blender

2. Set **Amount** to 0.02 m; this represents how large we're going to be affecting the corners of our cube object. Basically, the one corner edge we got by default will be divided into two edges, and the distance between the two edges is the bevel amount.

3. Set **Segments** to 3; this indicates how many face loops there are going to be inside the bevel.

4. Select the beveled cube, then right-click and choose **Smooth**.

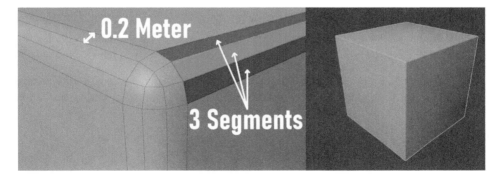

Figure 1.21 – Three cubes demonstrating the Amount, Segments, and Smooth bevel settings

The other cube will remain as default: no beveling will be applied.

When you add a source of light to the scene, you will see a big difference between the two cubes:

Figure 1.22 – Final render of the beveled and unbeveled cubes

The red beveled cube reflects light on its corners, which makes it more realistic. On the other hand, the blue cube looks fake right on the spot: its edges are 100% sharp and non-realistic.

In general, 3D software programs like Blender make everything perfect by default. When creating a cube, for example, it will come with these sharp 90-degree corners, something that doesn't exist in real life. In nature, you'll never find an object that has completely sharp edges. Even if you zoom in on a sharp knife (zoom really close to its edge), you'll find some sort of beveling.

I've heard a saying that says, "*Imperfection is the CGI perfection*," which means that in order to make objects photorealistic, we have to break the perfection that comes with CGI, and one of the first steps to break it is to *always apply the bevel modifier*.

Now with the measurements we set earlier and the help of the fSpy, we can set the right scale.

Summary

In this chapter, we went through the three modeling mistakes and how to fix them. Starting with scale matching, we discussed why it's a bad habit to rely on eyes only when modeling, how the Blender unit system works, and how to set the right measurements of objects before modeling them.

Next, we installed and configured the open source fSpy to help us match the same proportions of a real wood cabin reference, following which we learned how to install the fSpy add-on and import the fSpy file into Blender and built the basic scene that resembles the real reference scale.

Finally, we discussed the importance of using the bevel modifier and why it's crucial to achieving photorealism.

In the next chapter, we will be covering the second building block for photorealism, which is the creation of PBR materials. We will break down the components of PBR materials and understand the role of each channel and how it works. Finally, we will create an example of realistic wood material in Blender using procedural texturing.

2

The Basics of Realistic Texturing in Blender

Materials are the holy grail for achieving **photorealism**. If we have only 10 hours to spend on a scene to make it photorealistic, I would say you need to probably put at least 5 to 6 hours into materials – that's more than 50% of the work. Yes, materials are that important.

We can get away with some modeling mistakes: the scale can be 90% off and we can get away with it. But with materials, if the shading and textures don't match that of real-world materials, our scene will be screaming *fake*. There is something about the way the light hits an object; if the object is a piece of wood, the light will behave differently than when it hits a metal bar.

In this chapter, we will highlight the importance of using all texturing channels in achieving photorealism by showing examples of realistic materials and breaking them down into their components: Base Color, Roughness, Normal, and Displacement. You will gain an understanding of each one of these maps and how they work inside **Blender**.

In this chapter, we'll cover the following topics:

- Exploring the components for achieving photorealistic texturing: Base Color, Roughness, Normal, and Displacement
- Creating a realistic wood material using procedural texturing in Blender

Technical requirements

This chapter requires a Mac or PC capable of running Blender Version 3.0 or above.

You can download the resources for this chapter from GitHub at `https://github.com/PacktPublishing/3D-Environment-Design-with-Blender/tree/main/chapter-2`

Exploring the components for achieving photorealistic texturing in Blender

When we start texturing in Blender, most of us do it the simple way: you search for an image texture, create a simple material, jump into the *Shader Editor*, and assign it to **Base Color** under **Principled BSDF**, and that's it.

> Principled BSDF
>
> **Principled BSDF** is a node we get in Blender by default; it includes multiple layers that allow us to create a wide variety of materials just by tweaking values.

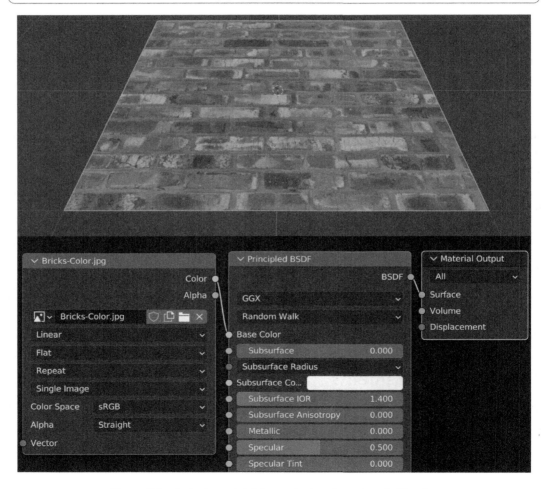

Figure 2.1 – Assigning a brick image texture to a plane in Blender

You can get away with it, but it's the wrong way to treat materials.

This simple texturing method looks flat and boring compared to alternative methods available, where the bricks look more realistic and pleasing to the eye. You can see the difference in the following figure:

Figure 2.2 – Comparison between wrong texturing and realistic texturing in Blender

Back when I started, I always thought that the depth details you see on the bricks shown in the image on the right-hand side of *Figure 2.2* were actually real geometry, but eventually, I figured out that it's just a texturing trick that makes objects look much more realistic.

If we want to achieve photorealistic texturing, we need to provide Blender with multiple pieces of information about the material we're creating. We need to define how it looks: its color; how shiny it is; whether it is wet, rough, dry, or smooth; the amount of bumps the material has; and the height of the material. All these details are represented in images: some call them maps or channels.

Figure 2.3 – Base Color, Roughness, Normal, and Displacement maps

Let me walk you through the different maps available that help in the process of creating photorealistic bricks.

The Base Color map

The first map is the **Base Color** map; this is fairly obvious. It represents the surface color of the material and it's the first thing we see in our material. When you assign the **Base Color** map in the *Shader Editor*, you will see the same result as on the left-hand side of *Figure 2.2*: flat and boring. It's like printing an image of bricks onto paper. Stopping here is a mistake most of us make in the beginning, and as you can see in the left sphere of *Figure 2.2*, the brick material is nowhere close to photorealism.

To assign the **Base Color** map, on a brand-new Blender scene, do the following:

1. Create a simple plane using *Shift + A* on the 3D Viewport, then choose **Mesh** and **Plane**.
2. From the right panel, click on the **Material Properties** icon.
3. You can change the material name to Bricks.

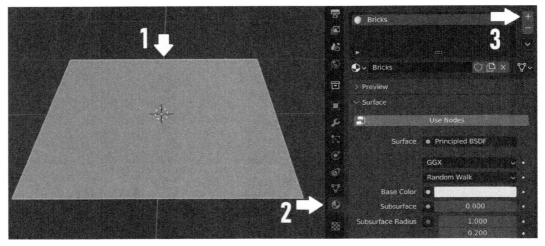

Figure 2.4 – Creating a plane with wood material applied to it

Now let's jump into the Shader Editor. At the bottom, by default, we'll have the **Timeline**. We need to switch to the *Shader Editor*, where you can work and make changes to your materials by using nodes.

We'll be using the bricks image shown in *Figure 2.7* to texture our plane shown in *Figure 2.5*; this bricks image is available at https://github.com/PacktPublishing/ Photorealistic-3D-Nature-Environment-Creation-with-Blender/ blob/2a43699e9eb017f7b0b0b54cb0adb083f4038f18/chapter-2/Brick_Color. jpg.

You can save this image on your desktop.

Now, let's expand the bottom bar to see what's inside; you can do so by grabbing it from the edge and moving it up. Now, if you select the plane, you will see two nodes: **Principled BSDF** and **Material Output**. This means you're on the right track.

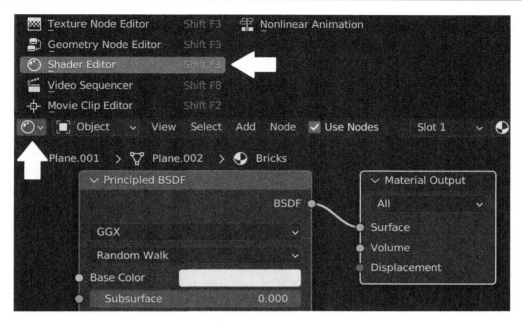

Figure 2.5 – Switching the Timeline to Shader Editor

The first element in the **Principled BSDF** node that is connectable is the **Base Color** map. You can connect the first element in **Principled BDSF** as follows: drag the **Brick_Color.jpg** texture from your desktop and drop it into the *Shader Editor* in Blender. You will see it as an image texture node. Now, we need to connect the **Color** yellow point with **Base Color** on the **Principled BSDF** node.

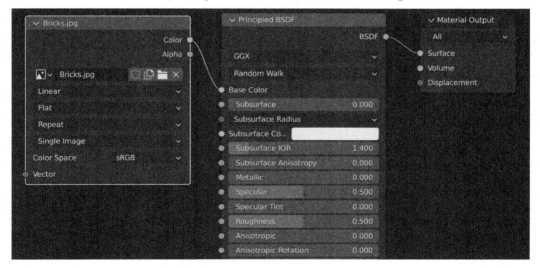

Figure 2.6 – Three nodes in the Shader Editor – brick image texture, Principled BSDF, and Material Output

However, we still do not observe any change. This is because we're in **Solid** mode by default. This mode shows everything in gray. In order to see the materials applied to our object, we need to switch to the **Material Preview** mode. Place your mouse on top of the plane, press Z, and switch to **Material Preview**:

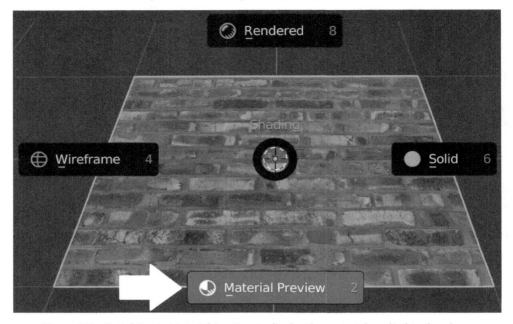

Figure 2.7 – Switching to Material Preview to display the material applied to the plane

Immediately, you will see the texture of the bricks applied to the plane. This is the first step we take to texture an object in Blender but we should not stop here. We need to give Blender more details about our material in order to achieve photorealism, which brings us to the **Roughness map**.

The Roughness map

The Roughness map controls the reflection of the material. It's a black and white image that allows us to control how shiny or rough our material is: black means shiny, whereas white means rough.

When we assign the Roughness map to our material, any black surface will be displayed as shiny, whereas white surfaces will be translated to rough surfaces.

To explain how Blender handles the Roughness map, let's perform this simple experiment:

1. Choose any **paint** software you have on your computer; I'll be using the Paint software on Windows.

2. Try painting some black puddles on a white surface – something like this:

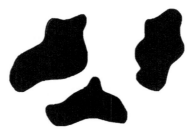

Figure 2.8 – Image with three black puddles used to demonstrate how the Roughness map works

3. Now, back to the Blender scene, we have the bricks texture assigned to **Base Color**; let's disconnect it temporarily, and instead, let's drag and drop the black puddles image into the *Shader Editor* and connect it to **Roughness** in the **Principled BSDF** node.

4. Also, to see the effect more clearly, make sure to change the color of the **Base Color** map to black. You'll obtain the following result:

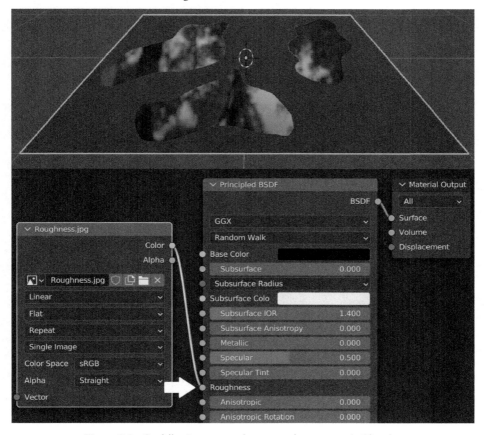

Figure 2.9 – Puddles image used as a roughness map in Blender

You can see that the black spots are completely glossy, while the white spots are rough. You can delete the puddles image by selecting the image node and pressing *X*.

This is how the Roughness map works.

This is the brick Roughness map we'll be using. You can get it from this link: `https://github.com/PacktPublishing/3D-Environment-Design-with-Blender/blob/2a43699e9eb017f7b0b0b54cb0adb083f4038f18/chapter-2/Brick_Roughness.jpg`

After downloading the `Brick-Roughness.jpg` texture, drop it in the **Shader Editor** and assign it to the **Principled BSDF | Roughness** slot as the following screenshot shows:

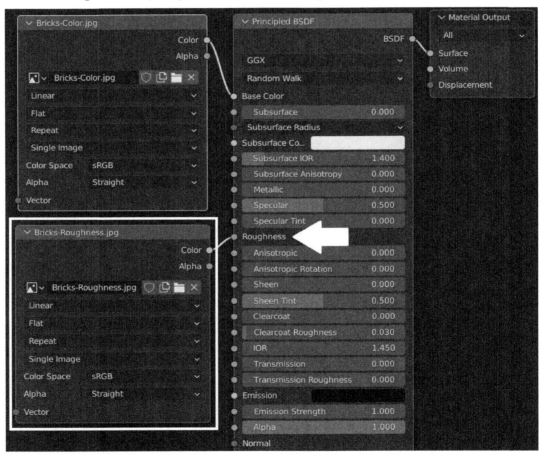

Figure 2.10 – Assigning the Brick Roughness image to the Roughness slot of the Principled BSDF

After assigning the **Brick-Roughness.jpg** texture to **Roughness** in the **Principled BSDF** slot, we need to change the **Color Space** type of the roughness texture from **sRGB** to **Non-Color**. The roughness should not be not treated as color; we do this to avoid any possible color transforms.

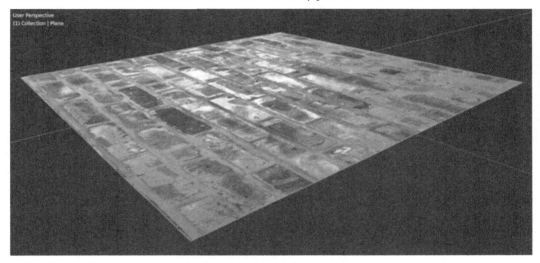

Figure 2.11 – Assigning the Roughness map to the bricks material

Alright, the preceding screenshot shows the result of the bricks material when we added the Roughness map. The next step is to apply the **Normal map**.

> **Remember**
> When dealing with the Roughness map, black means reflective and white means rough.

The Normal map

Have you ever seen bluish images in the texturing process and wondered what their use is?

Figure 2.12 – Example of a Normal map

This is a Normal map, and when you apply it to a 3D object, it creates the illusion of height. It adds free detail that costs us nothing in terms of performance; more specifically, it does not affect the render time and adds significant detail and realism to the object it's applied to. Gaming companies heavily use this method to maximize rendering performance while maintaining a photorealistic look.

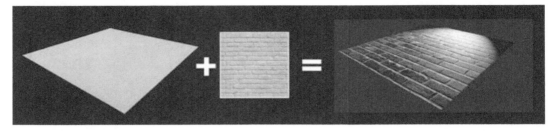

Figure 2.13 – Applying a brick Normal map to a plane

Now, let's apply a normal map to our bricks example. To do that, we'll need a new node called **Normal Map**. So, place the cursor on the *Shader Editor*, press *Shift + A*, search for Normal Map, and press *Enter*. The **Normal Map** node looks like this:

Figure 2.14 – An image of the Normal Map node

To use this node, we need to connect the **Brick_Normal** image texture to the **Normal Map Color** slot.

The Normal map texture we'll be using is available here for download: https://github.com/PacktPublishing/3D-Environment-Design-with-Blender/blob/2a43699e9eb017f7b0b0b54cb0adb083f4038f18/chapter-2/Brick_Normal.jpg.

Then, on the other side, connect **Normal** to **Normal** on the **Principled BSDF** node. Immediately you'll see the bump effect on the brick's material, as shown in *Figure 2.17*:

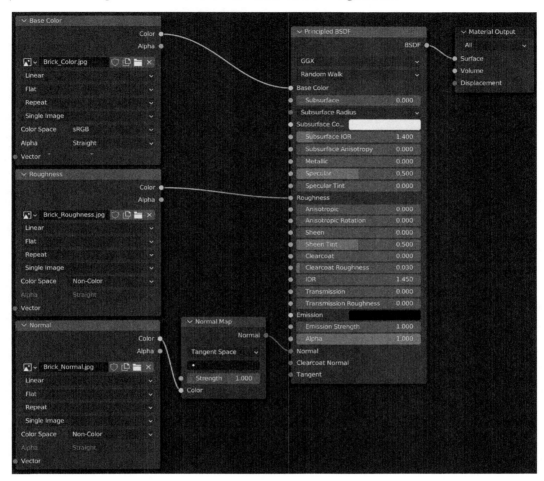

Figure 2.15 – Connecting the Brick Normal image texture to the Normal
Map node then to the Principled BSDF Normal slot

Now, with the **Normal Map** node applied, our material looks much more realistic. The plane now has free details that do not affect rendering performance:

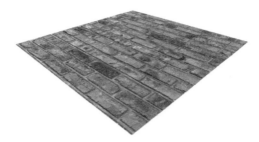

Figure 2.16 – Bricks texture with normal map applied

The next step is to explain the Displacement map.

The Displacement map

The Displacement map is a black and white image, similar to the Roughness map, but the role it plays is different. Think of it as an alternative way of modeling: we feed Blender a black and white image, and it puts it on top of a 3D object. The white spots are going to be pushed out or made to extrude, while the black spots are going to be pushed inward. The gray is neutral; it makes the geometry flat.

There is nothing better than an easy example to understand how the Displacement map works. I've created this simple design using *Paint*:

Figure 2.17 – Black image with white geometrical shape in the middle

If we apply this image to a plane as a **Height map**, it will look like this:

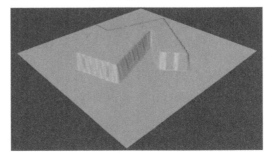

Figure 2.18 – Height map of image shown in Figure 2.17 applied to a plane

So, as you can see, the Height map deforms the shape of the mesh it's applied to; this is an actual geometry change. While a Normal map only modifies the lighting across the surface of a texture without deforming the geometry, the **Displacement map** goes a step further and actually modifies the shape of the mesh it's applied to.

The amount of extrusion depends on the intensity of white and black colors; black in the height map represents the lowest point on the plane, white represents the highest point on the plane, and gray indicates a height of 0. The following example explains this point:

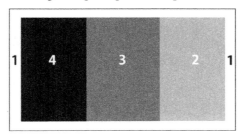

Figure 2.19 – Gradient colors:black, gray, and light gray

If we apply this image, which has four colors—black (4), gray (3), light gray (2), and white (1)—as a height map to our plane, we'll get the following result:

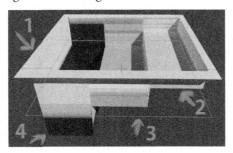

Figure 2.20 – Height map of Figure 2.19 applied to a plane

The white borders represented in the Displacement map are translated into the highest surface point on our plane.

The second light-gray color gives us an extrusion of only 50%

The third gray color gives us a flat 0% height detail; it's on the same level as the plane.

The fourth black color gives us a 100% extrusion downward.

Later, in the coming chapters, we will learn how to apply and use the Displacement map.

Now that we have learned how the Base Color, Roughness, Normal, and Height maps work, let's put everything together and create a realistic wood material to be applied to the wood cabin.

Creating a realistic wood material using procedural texturing in Blender

Let's apply everything we have learned so far to create various wood materials using procedural-generated texturing and apply it to our wooden cabin created in *Chapter 1, Most Common Modeling Mistakes That Prevent You from Achieving Photorealism.*

Let's begin by understanding procedural texturing in Blender.

Procedural texturing is the process of creating textures within Blender itself by using a collection of node textures that are defined mathematically. This is nice because it allows us to create high-quality textures without relying on external textures.

Let's set the Blender scene first:

1.   Create a new plane.

2.   Assign a new material to the plane and name it Wood.

3.   Switch the bottom panel to the *Shader Editor*.

4.   On the 3D Viewport, switch to *Material Preview* using *Z* in order to see the progress of our material.

Make sure you're selecting the plane in order to see the **Principled BSDF** and **Material Output** nodes. Now we're good to go:

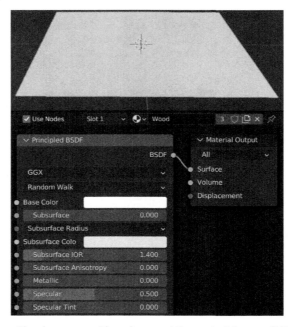

Figure 2.21 – New Blender scene with a plane and the material named Wood applied to it

If we want to create a wood texture, we need to understand the nature of wood itself; this will help us use the right nodes to create the wood texture:

Figure 2.22 – Wood image texture reference

The preceding figure is a real reference to a wood texture; if we pay close attention, we'll find that wood is a combination of small layers that are stretched. So, how can we replicate that in Blender?

The node that will allow us to make random layers is called **Musgrave Texture**. To obtain this node, press *Shift + A* on the *Shader Editor*, click on **Search**, and type Musgrave:

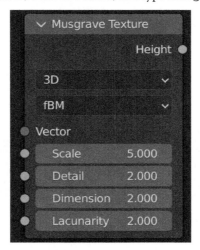

Figure 2.23 – Image of Musgrave Texture

So, here's the trick, we'll be combining two **Musgrave Texture** nodes in a row, one after the other, and connecting them to **Base Color**.

The scale of the first **Musgrave Texture** node should be set to the default value of 5, and the scale of the second **Musgrave Texture** node should be set to 50. This should obtain the following result:

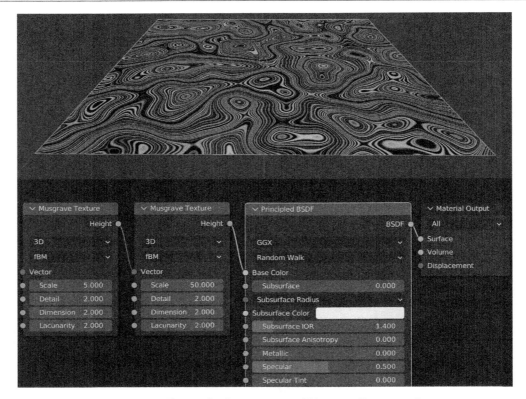

Figure 2.24 – The result of two connected Musgrave Texture nodes

We create layers similar to what you'll see in wood, but we need to add another effect, which is stretching. We need to stretch our texture to make it look more like wood. To accomplish this task, we'll be using two nodes, **Mapping** and **Texture Coordinate**:

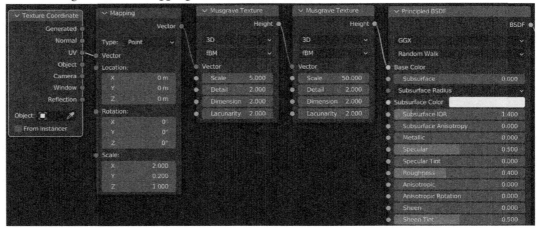

Figure 2.25 – Changing the scale of the wood texture

Let's connect the **UV** slot of the **Texture Coordinate** node to the **Vector** slot in the **Mapping** node; then connect the **Vector** slot of the **Mapping** node to the first **Musgrave Texture Vector** slot.

These two nodes allow us to move, rotate, and scale any texture it's connected to.

The first node, **Texture Coordinate**, defines the type of changes you want to make, so we set it to the UVs of the plane. The second node, **Mapping**, gives us three settings to change: the XYZ location of our texture, the XYZ rotation, and the XYZ scale.

The scale settings are on the X and Y axes. X is set to 0.2, and Y is set to 2. The following figure is the result of our wood texture so far:

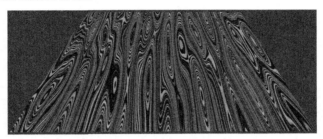

Figure 2.26 – Stretching the wood procedural texture using the Mapping node

As you can see, our result is starting to resemble actual wood.

The next step is to add a noise effect on the surface. If we zoom into the texture, it will look CG-perfect, so we need to add a noise effect to break up the perfection in our wood texture. So we need to add the **Noise Texture** node: to obtain this node, press *Shift + A* on the *Shader Editor*, click on Search, and type Noise Texture:

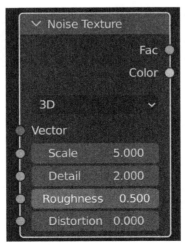

Figure 2.27 – Noise Texture node

If we connect the **Noise Texture** node to the **Base Color slot of the Principled BSDF**, this is how Noise Texture looks when applied on its own to a plane:

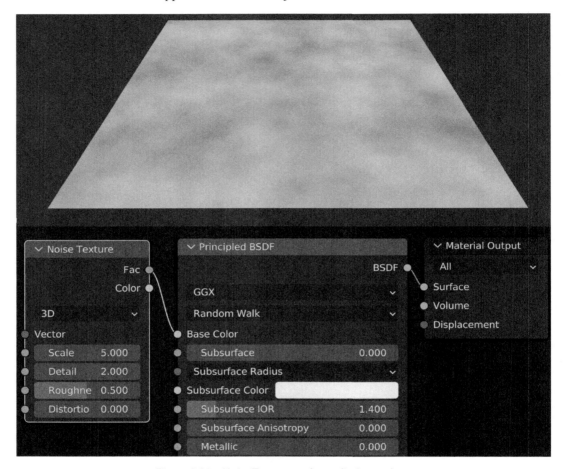

Figure 2.28 – Noise Texture node applied to a plane

We need to find a way to mix the **Noise Texture** node with the double **Musgrave Texture node**. The way to do it is to use a new node called **Mix**.

The Mix node

On the **Shader Editor**, press *Shift + A* and search for MixRGB; press *Enter* and you'll get the following node:

Figure 2.29 – Mix node

This node has three slots:

- **Fac**: Its value is between 0 and 1, this value controls the mixing amount. 0 means 100% of Color1, 1 means 100% of Color2.

- **Color1**: First node to mix.

- **Color2:** Second node to mix.

We use this node to mix two textures together. The **Fac** value controls the mixture amount: if you set it to 0, you will get 100% of the first texture assigned to the **Color1** slot; if you set it to 1, you will get 100% of the **Color2** slot. Putting it at 0.5, as seen in the preceding screenshot, will mix both colors fifty-fifty.

Let's use this **Mix** node to mix the **Noise Texture** node with the **Musgrave Texture** node:

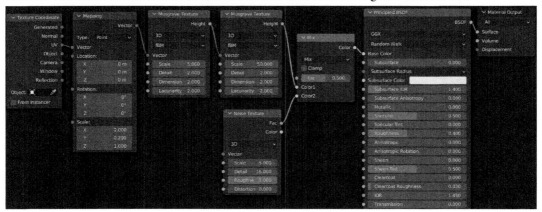

Figure 2.30 – Node setup in the Shader Editor of wood texture

I've made the following tweaks to the **Noise Texture** node:

- Increased the **Detail** slot amount to 16
- Set the **Roughness** slot amount to 1

This way we'll make the noise richer in detail, and smaller in size. This is what our wood material looks like now:

Figure 2.31 – Procedural wood texture

Now that we have the shape of the wood established, as you might guess, the next step will be to make our wood colorful; this is actually quite simple. Let's use the **ColorRamp** node again.

Adding color to the wood texture using the ColorRamp node

As I said, the next step will be to make our wood colorful; we'll be using the **ColorRamp** node again. Press *Shift + A* on the *Shader Editor*, search for ColorRamp, and drop it between the **Mix** and the **Principled BSDF** nodes; it will automatically connect to the node group:

1. Select the right thumb on the track bar and move it toward a light brown color.
2. Add a new thumb using the **plus** icon at the top of the **ColorRamp** node window (2).
3. Change the color of the new thumb to a darker brown color (3).

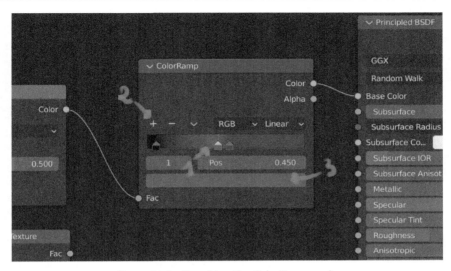

Figure 2.32 – Tweaking the ColorRamp node

I highly suggest you keep playing with this **ColorRamp** node; it will give you excellent control over the color of your material – you can change it to any color you want. This is the beauty of using procedural texturing in Blender: making textures is 100% flexible.

With the tweaks to the **ColorRamp** node, this is what our wood texture now looks like:

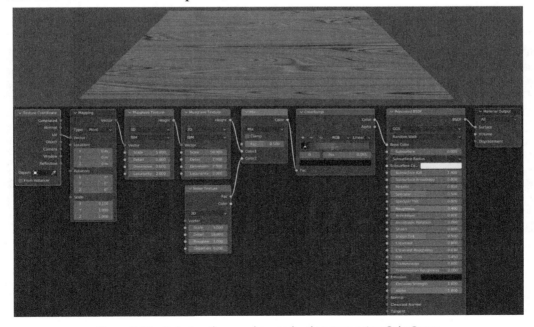

Figure 2.33 – Coloring the wood procedural texture using ColorRamp

You can see the new changes I made to the **ColorRamp** node, and as a result, I got a new wood look:

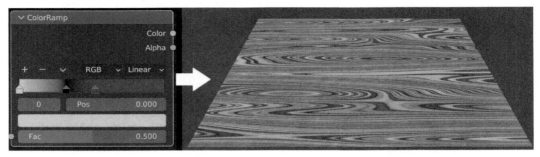

Figure 2.34 – Changing the settings of ColorRamp to get a different wood texture

Now that we have finished working on the first channel of our wood material, the Base Color, we need other details because, as you know, our wood material is flat and unrealistic right now. We need to add other details like the roughness that controls the reflection and the normal that adds bumps to the surface.

Adding wood reflection using the Roughness map

To work on the wood reflection, we need to add a **ColorRamp** node and connect the output of the previous **ColorRamp** node that controls the color of the wood to the new **ColorRamp** node and tweak the thumbs on the track bar.

You can see the **wood** node setup maximized in the following screenshot:

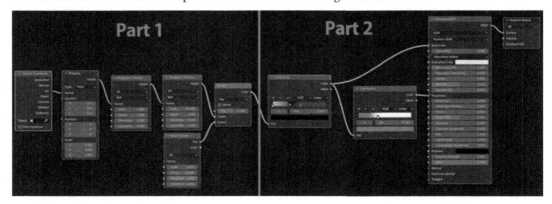

Figure 2.35 – Full node setup for wood material

I've divided the image into two parts so that you can see the minor details. This is part 1 of the wood node setup:

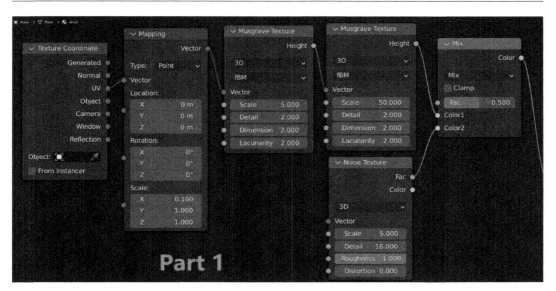

Figure 2.36 – Part 1 of the wood node setup

This is part 2 of the wood node setup:

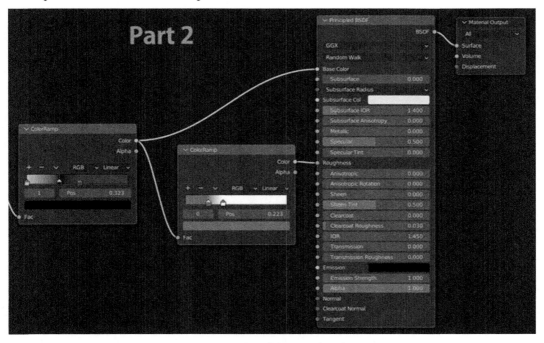

Figure 2.37 – Part 2 of the wood node setup

Here is the final result, showing reflectivity added to the wood:

Figure 2.38 – Adding reflectivity to the wood material

Now we can see the reflection variation we have in our wood material. The next step is to add bumps to the surface.

Adding bumps to the surface of the wood material

So far, we have the color of the wood and the nice reflection on the surface, but our material still looks flat and non-realistic. We need to add the bumps to make it photorealistic.

For this, let's add the **Bump** node and put it between **Color** in the **ColorRamp** node and **Normal** in the **Principled BSDF** node, just as seen in the following figure:

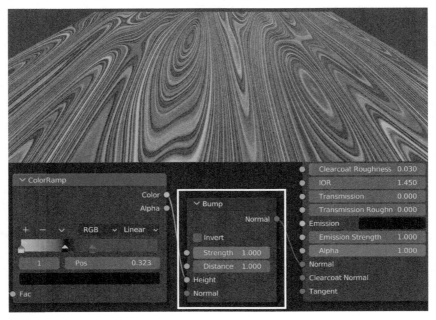

Figure 2.39 – Adding the Bump node to make the wood surface bumpy

Now we can see the bumps on the surface of our wood material; however, we need to reduce the **Strength** slot of the **Bump** node down to something around 0.1 in order to make our wood look more realistic:

Figure 2.40 – Reducing the strength of the Bump node to 0.1

And congratulations! We have created a realistic wood material that can be used later to texture our wood cabin.

Summary

In this chapter, we first went through the basics of realistic texturing in Blender by breaking down the four components of a realistic material: the **Base Color** map, the Roughness map for the reflectivity of our material, the Normal map for the bumps on the surface, and the Height map that changes the real shape of the mesh geometry.

Then, we created a wood material using procedural texturing in Blender. We used a combination of nodes, such as **Musgrave Texture**, **Noise Texture**, **Mix**, **Mapping**, and **Texture Coordinate**, to create a realistic wood material.

In the next chapter, we will focus on UV mapping in Blender and how to do it the right way in order to maximize photorealism. We will apply the wood texture we created to the wood cabin. This will enable you to understand the art of unwrapping 3D objects.

3

Efficient Unwrapping and Texturing in Blender

Unwrapping is an essential skill for applying textures to 3D objects. Therefore, in this chapter, we will understand what exactly unwrapping is and why it is needed, as well as the tools and techniques required to help you efficiently map your 3D objects in Blender. You will be doing a whole lot of unwrapping of models that have different shapes and sizes and then texturing them. The goal here is to unwrap and texture our wood cabin model.

In this chapter, we'll be covering the following topics:

- Importing the wood material
- Unwrapping and texturing our wood cabin

Technical requirements

This chapter requires a Mac or PC capable of running Blender Version 3.0 or above.

You can download the resources for this chapter from GitHub at `https://github.com/PacktPublishing/3D-Environment-Design-with-Blender/tree/main/chapter-3`

Importing the wood material

In the previous chapter, we created a wood material using procedural texturing. Now, it's time to apply it to the wood cabin model that you will find in the resources to download, which is available at `https://github.com/PacktPublishing/3D-Environment-Design-with-Blender/tree/main/chapter-3`.

After downloading the wood cabin model, we need to unwrap it first and texture it. To do so, first, let's import the wood material we created in the previous chapter and use it inside the Wood Cabin Model Blender file:

1. Click on **File** and choose **Append**:

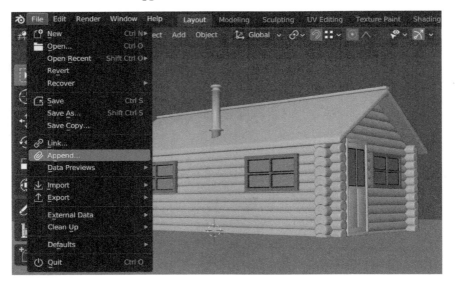

Figure 3.1 – Importing files from other scenes using Append

2. Then, select the Blender file (Wood.blend) where you created the wood material.

    You will see a window asking you what type of folder you want to import from the Blender file you selected:

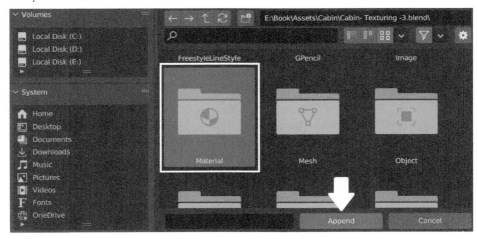

Figure 3.2 – Choosing the type of file to import in Blender

Here, Blender allows us to import anything from the Blender file we chose. In our case, we want a material.

3. Double-click on the **Material** folder (highlighted in blue in the preceding figure); you should find the wood material you created.

4. Select it and click on **Append**.

    Now, the wood material is appended.

If you want to check that you have the wood material, go to the *Materials Properties* (*step 1* in the following figure) and then click on the **Materials repository** (*step 2* in the following figure). Here you will find all the materials you have in the scene, and **Wood** will be one of them.

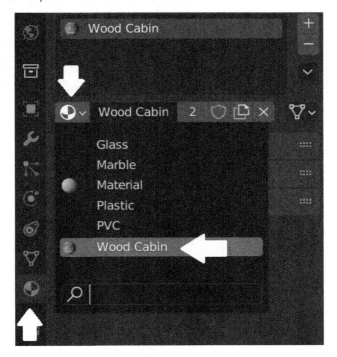

Figure 3.3 – Materials repository in Material properties

Now that we've imported our wood material into the new wood cabin model Blender scene, let's go ahead and assign it to the wood cabin.

Texturing our wood cabin

Let's texture the wood cabin using the imported wood material:

1. Select the front of the wood cabin.

2. Go to **Material Properties**, you will find it empty; this means that the selected object has no material attached to it.

3. Click on the **Material repository** and select the **Wood Cabin** material we imported to our scene:

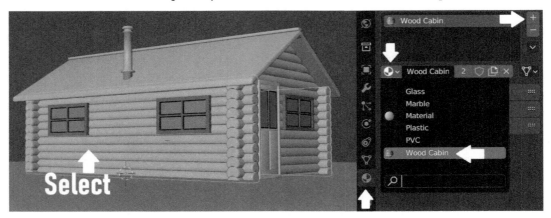

Figure 3.4 – Assigning wood material to the wood cabin

Now, the wood material is applied to the front of the cabin, but we can't see it because the Viewport Display is set to `Solid`. The Viewport Display refers to the overall look of the 3D Viewport. We need to switch the Viewport Display to **Material Preview** to see the material applied to our objects. So, hover your mouse on the 3D Viewport, press *Z*, and choose **Material Preview**:

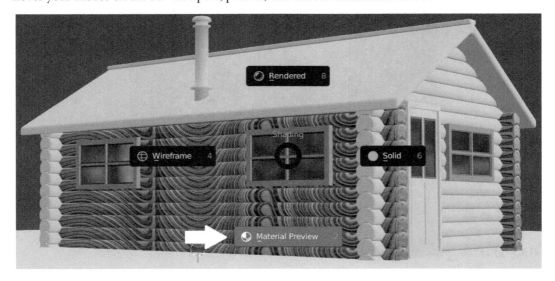

Figure 3.5 – Switching to Material Preview to see the wood material

The current wood texture looks repetitive and non-realistic; this has to do with the bad unwrapping of our cabin.

We need to better unwrap our wood cabin to have more control over how we want the wood material to be displayed. To understand what's happening here, let's break down UV mapping.

What is UV mapping?

Before texturing our wood cabin, let's understand what UV mapping is. UV mapping or unwrapping – both terms refer to the same thing – is the process of wrapping a 2D image texture onto a 3D mesh. **U** and **V** are the names of the axes in the UV Editor, while X, Y, and Z refer to the coordinates in the 3D Viewport.

By default, meshes are created with UVs, meaning that when you add a mesh, Blender will automatically unwrap it and generate UVs in the UV Editor.

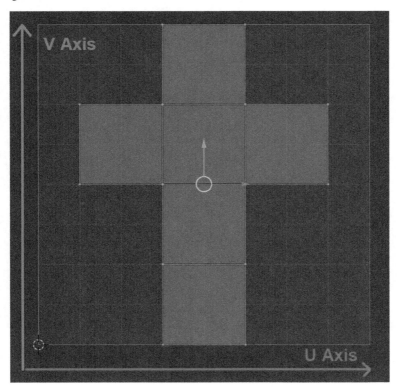

Figure 3.6 – U and V axes displayed in the UV Editor

To understand unwrapping better, let's take an example: I've created a simple cube (shown in *Figure 3.7*). Imagine you're holding a pair of scissors and cutting the cube – we've all done this in our childhood. To get a perfect cube and lay it down, we need to make seven cuts to the edges highlighted in green. To do so, press the *Tab* key to switch to Edit Mode, select the highlighted green edges, press *Ctrl + E*, and choose **Mark Seam**. This means you're marking the edges for Blender to cut:

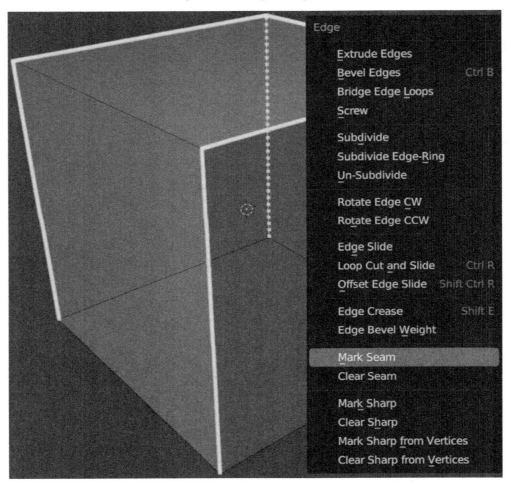

Figure 3.7 – Marking seams of a cube to unwrap it

Next, to unwrap our cube, press *U* while selecting the cube in Edit Mode. You will get a menu; select **Unwrap**. Let's expand the timeline window and switch it to **UV Editor**:

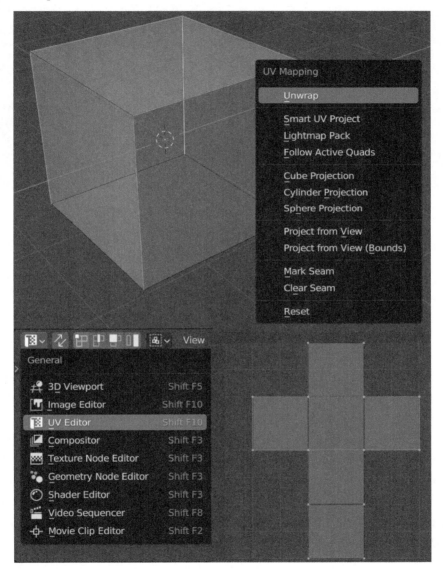

Figure 3.8 – Unwrapping a cube and seeing the UV map in the UV Editor

We can see the UV map displayed in the UV Editor. The next step is to export the UV map as an image. On the top bar, you will find a **UV** tab (*step 1* in the following figure); click on it and select **Export UV Layout** (*step 2*):

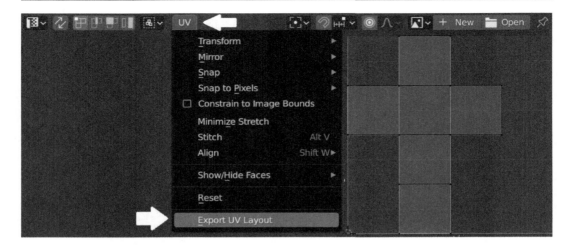

Figure 3.9 – Exporting the UV layout of the cube UV map

Then, you can save the UV layout and open it in any image editor – I'll be using *Paint* in Windows. Fill each box with a different color and add numbers:

Figure 3.10 – Texturing the cube UV layout

In the last box, I've put a wood texture to show you, as an example, that you can put anything you want. Save the UV layout to your desktop; we'll be using it later.

Now, back to our Blender scene; let's wrap this texture around our cube. To do that, we need to create a material and assign it to the cube. Select the cube, click on **Material Properties**, and select **New Material**. Also, make sure to switch the bottom window from **UV Editor** to **Shader Editor** to tweak the cube material.

With the cube selected in **Shader Editor**, you will see the **Principled BSDF** node. We need to first drag the texture we have in *Figure 3.10* from your desktop and drop it in the **Shader Editor**. The texture will turn automatically into an image texture node (**Cube** node), just like in the following figure:

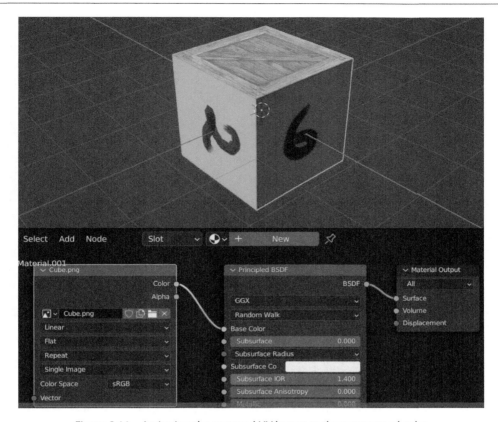

Figure 3.11 – Assigning the textured UV layout to the unwrapped cube

Now, to assign the texture shown in *Figure 3.10* to our cube, all we have to do then is connect the cube texture node to **Base Color** of the **Principled BSDF** node and switch the 3D Viewport to **Material Preview** by pressing Z. Then, you will see the texture we created in *Figure 3.10* wrapped around the cube as shown in *Figure 3.11* above.

This is the right way to unwrap and texture 3D objects. Back to our wood cabin, the shape of the wall is multiple cylinders, one on top of the other; let's unwrap them.

Unwrapping the wood cabin

We'll be doing the same thing we did with the cube to the wood cylinders. Let's unwrap the cylinders!

Unwrapping the cylinders

Unwrapping cylinders is easy. Again, imagine you're holding a pair of scissors to cut a cylinder and then laying it on the floor: we first need to cut the side circles of the cylinder and then make a cut through the cylinder, just like the seams highlighted in red in the following figure:

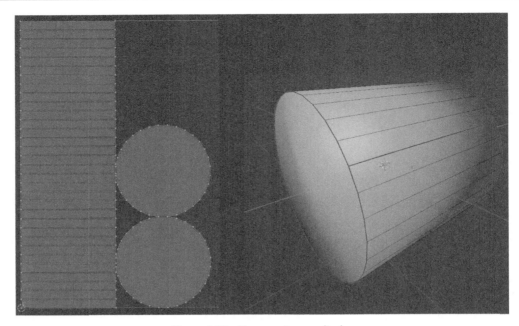

Figure 3.12 – Unwrapping a cylinder

Then, select the wood cylinder, and select an edge from the bottom with the circle cut on the end. Press *Ctrl + E* and choose **Mark Seam**:

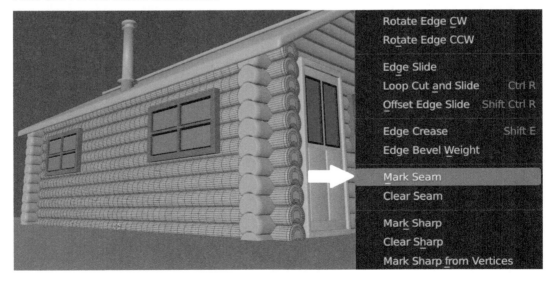

Figure 3.13 – Marking seams of the wood cabin cylinders

To unwrap the wood cylinders, select them all, press *U*, and choose **Unwrap**. If you switch to the **Material Preview** mode by pressing *Z*, you will see that the wood looks better and random, but the texture will appear large; we need to scale up the UVs to cover a large portion of the texture. To do that, let's go back to the *Shader Editor* and add the **Mapping** node along with the **Texture Coordinate** node, which will control the size of the wood texture. We did the same in *Chapter 2, The Basics of Realistic Texturing in Blender* (*Figure 2.26*). I have scaled up the wood texture five times. Here, I set the **X** axis to 0.5 and the **Y** axis to 5:

Figure 3.14 – Scaling up the wood texture using the Mapping node

Do the same thing to the other wood sides. Once done, let's work on the roof.

Unwrapping and texturing the roof

To texture the roof, let's perform the following steps:

1. Select the roof, go to **Material Properties**, and create a new material called Roof. Save the roof texture, which is available at https://github.com/PacktPublishing/3D-Environment-Design-with-Blender/blob/main/chapter-3/Roof.jpg, on your desktop.

2. Drag and drop it into the **Shader Editor**.

3. Connect the **Color** slot of the roof texture node to **Base Color** of the **Principled BSDF** node in the **Shader Editor**, as shown in *Figure 3.16*.

    If we switch to **Material Preview**, the roof material won't be displayed properly (see *Figure 3.15*). So, we need a better way to unwrap it. Since the roof is not an important area, there is no need to spend a lot of time marking seams; instead, we will let Blender do it for us by using Smart UV Project.

Smart UV Project

Smart UV Project is an automatic method of unwrapping a mesh. If you choose this option, Blender will automatically place new seams and unwrap the mesh for you. While Smart UV Project might seem like an easy way to unwrap your objects, it often produces results that are less satisfactory than manual unwrapping. We only use it for simple objects, for example, our roof.

---

4. Select the roof, switch to **Edit Mode**, make sure that all the roof geometry is selected, press *U*, and choose **Smart UV Project**. Then, click **OK**.

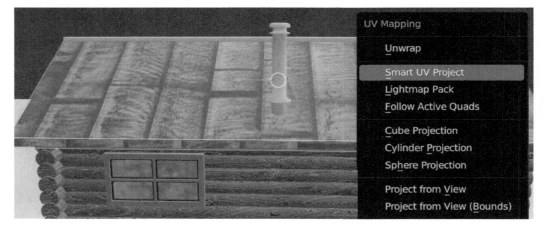

Figure 3.15 – Unwrapping the roof of the wood cabin

Note that this method doesn't work properly all the time, so it needs some tweaking. We have to switch the direction of the top roof texture to horizontal. To do that, let's jump into the **Shader Editor** to see the **Roof** material

5. Add the **Mapping** and **Texture Coordinate** nodes:

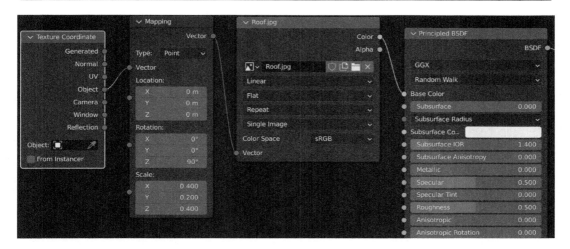

Figure 3.16 – Node setup of the wood cabin material

6.   In the **Mapping** node, you might have a different axis to change depending on the texture orientation, X or Y. Just keep an eye on the roof texture; also tweak its scale. In my case, I have changed the scale to 0.4 on both the X and Z axes, with 0.2 on the Y axis; I find that this setting works best. I highly advise you to tweak the **Rotation** and **Scale** values while checking the roof to understand how the **Mapping** node works.

Figure 3.17 – Texturing the roof of the wood cabin

Next, we need to tweak the material reflection – so far the roof looks like a flat painting.

7.   Let's add the **ColorRamp** node: connect **Color** in the roof texture node to **Fac** in the **ColorRamp** node and place the thumbs in the sliding bars as shown in *Figure 3.18* for better roof reflection.

8.   Let's also add the **Bump** node: connect the **Color** yellow slot from the roof texture node to the **Height** slot of the **Bump** node with 0.5 strength to have realistic details on our roof:

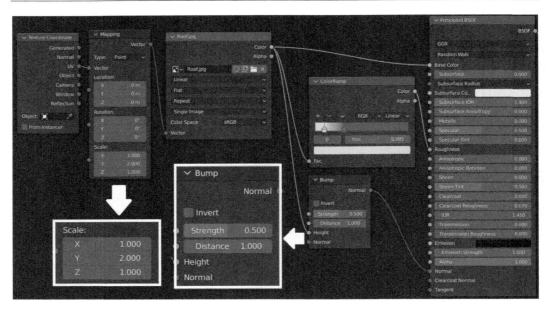

Figure 3.18 – Adding bumps and roughness to the roof material

This is how the roof looks now after applying the roof material we just created:

Figure 3.19 – Roof material texturing completed

Next, let's work on the metal chimney on the roof.

Texturing the chimney

To texture the chimney, we'll be using a metal texture to make it look like this:

Figure 3.20 – Texturing the chimney using a metal texture

1. Select the chimney object, and create a material called metal. Save the metal texture you will find available at https://github.com/PacktPublishing/Photorealistic-3D-Nature-Environment-Creation-with-Blender/blob/main/chapter-3/Metal.jpeg to your desktop.

2. Drag and drop it in the **Shader Editor**.

3. Connect the **Color** slot of the metal texture node to **Base Color** of the **Principled BSDF** node.

4. To make the material look like metal, increase the **Metallic** value on **Principled BSDF** to 0.9.

5. Add a **ColorRamp** node, and place the thumbs in the sliding bars as shown in *Figure 3.21* to make the metal material look reflective.

6. Add a **Bump** node and set the strength to a value of 0.1:

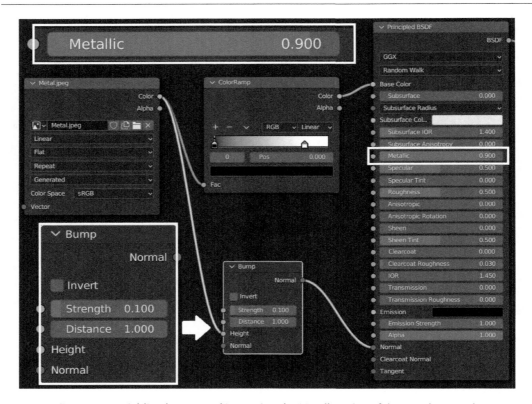

Figure 3.21 – Adding bumps and increasing the Metallic value of the metal material

You can see that the wood shape is 100% straight and non-realistic. This is impossible unless you cut the wood using a machine, and since the wood used in the cabin is organic, this means that its shape won't be perfect. So, we need to add some sort of imperfections to the shape of our wood to make it look real and similar to the reference.

Figure 3.22 – Metal chimney texturing completed

We can affect the geometry of the wood bars in the **Edit Mode**, but it will take a lot of time. Luckily, there is a better way to adjust the geometry using the Height map we learned about in the previous chapter. We will apply a cloud texture to the geometry and it will break the CGI perfection.

The cloud texture is a free texture provided by Blender, and it has white and dark spots. It can be used along with the **Displace** modifier to make an object's geometry distorted:

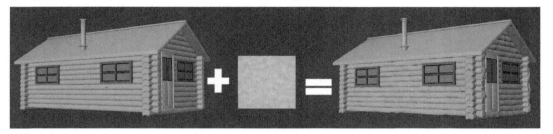

Figure 3.23 – Applying the cloud texture as a height map to the wood cabin model

To better understand how the **Displace** modifier works, think of a pin wall:

Figure 3.24 – Pin wall

The object you put through the wall is the displacement map: black areas are pushed while white areas remain flat. The pins here represent the subdivisions; the more pins you have, the clearer the object will be.

That's why we need to subdivide the wood geometry:

1. Press *Ctrl + E* and choose **Subdivide**. You can also add multiple edge loops using *Ctrl + R* and then scroll your mouse 10 to 15 times.

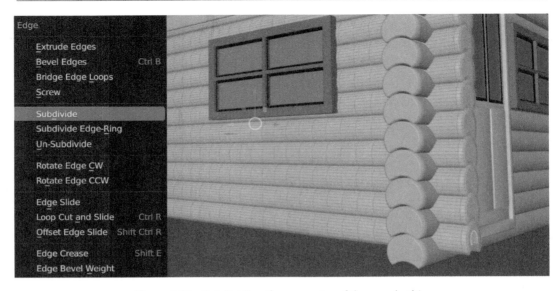

Figure 3.25 – Subdividing the geometry of the wood cabin

Now, let's add the **Displace** modifier to our wood cabin. The **Displace** modifier displaces vertices in a mesh based on the intensity of a texture.

2. Make sure you're selecting the wood cabin wall you want to apply the modifier to. On the right bar, you will find a **wrench** icon; click on it and select **Displace**:

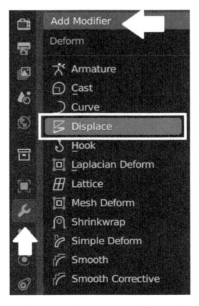

Figure 3.26 – Adding the Displace modifier to the wood cabin

The next step is to create the clouds texture to use it with the **Displace** modifier.

3. Click on the **Texture Properties** (the **checkerboard** icon) and select **New**, and for **Type**, choose **Clouds**:

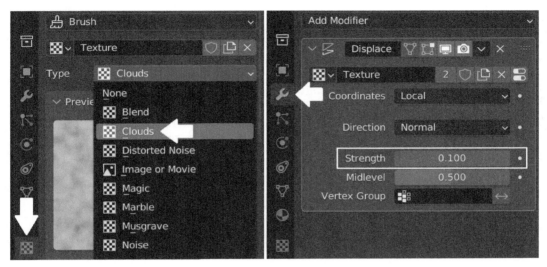

Figure 3.27 – Using the Cloud texture in the Displace modifier while reducing its strength

4. Change the strength of the **Displace** modifier to a value between 0.1 and 0.5, until you see a good displace effect; the result should be as follows:

Figure 3.28 – Final render of the wood cabin unwrapped and textured

Summary

In this chapter, we went through the process of unwrapping our wood cabin and texturing it in Blender. We started by learning how to import materials from one scene into another, followed by understanding how UV mapping works. We used the Displace modifier to add random details to the wood geometry.

Now, with the skills you've learned in this chapter, you can successfully unwrap any 3D object, import and assign materials to that 3D object, tweak the material nodes to make it fit the overall scene, and make the 3D object look realistic by applying displace imperfections.

In the next chapter, we'll focus on the surroundings of the wood cabin; we will learn how to create realistic, natural plants and trees, and use the particle system to randomly scatter plants around the wood cabin to enrich our natural environment.

4

Creating Realistic Natural Plants in Blender

In this chapter, you will learn to create a realistic natural scene with various plants and leaves in Blender. You'll learn how to model, texture, and place different types of plants in your environment. You will learn how to use the particle system in Blender to generate random plants in your scene.

In this chapter, we'll be covering the following topics:

- Creating realistic natural ground
- Creating plants and leaves

Technical requirements

This chapter requires a Mac or PC capable of running Blender Version 3.0 or above.

You can download the resources for this chapter from GitHub at https://github.com/PacktPublishing/3D-Environment-Design-with-Blender/tree/main/chapter-4

Modeling realistic natural ground

To create a realistic natural ground, let's follow these steps:

1. Add a plane under the wood cabin by pressing *Shift + A* on the 3D Viewport, and scale it 10 times by pressing *S* and typing 10 simultaneously in **Edit** mode:

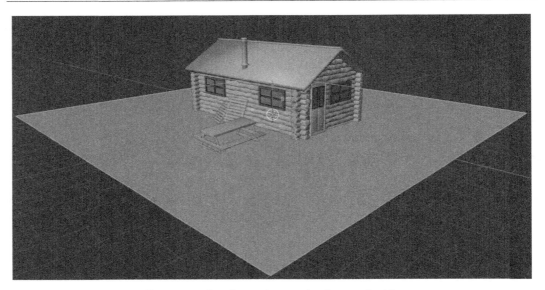

Figure 4.1 – Creating a plane under the wood cabin

Our plane looks 100% flat. We can add some bumps to our ground to break its perfection; as you know, in nature, there is no such thing as perfectly flat ground.

2. Select the plane, switch to **Edit** mode, press *Ctrl + E*, and choose **Subdivide**.

3. In the bottom left corner, you will find a **Subdivide** tab. Increase the **Number of Cuts** to 25:

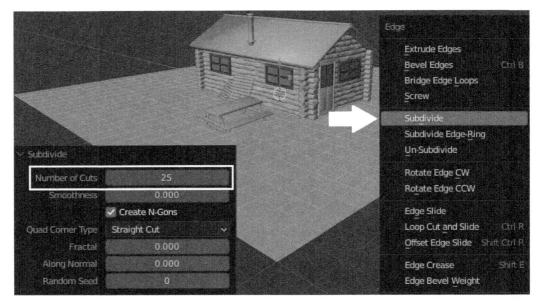

Figure 4.2 – Subdividing the plane 25 times

4. Let's use the **Proportional Editing** tool in the top bar of the 3D Viewport. It has an icon of a dot surrounded by a circle. Click on it to activate it. Also make sure that the mode you're using is **Smooth**:

Figure 4.3 – Enabling the Proportional Editing tool

Now, if we select three random points from our plane and raise them, we will see that we're making nice hills on our ground. You can change the size of the circle that appears in the middle by scrolling your mouse up or down. This affects the number of vertices around the selected vertices.

> **Note**
>
> I advise you to try different modes, such as Sharp and Linear, and see the effect they have on the geometry.

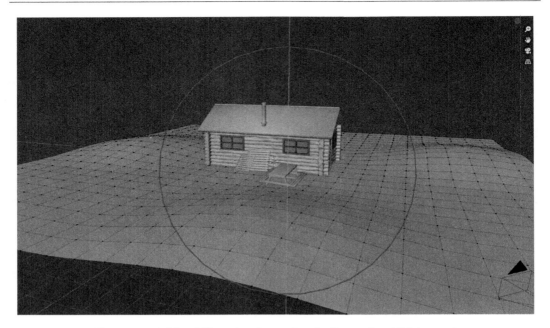

Figure 4.4 – Adding hills to the plane using the Proportional Editing tool

The goal here is to break the perfection of the plane so it's not 100% flat anymore. Now, let's go ahead and create plants and leaves to naturally enrich our environment.

Creating the plants and leaves

Let's look at how to do this:

1. To create plants, first we need to download the leaves reference, which is available at https://github.com/PacktPublishing/3D-Environment-Design-with-Blender/blob/main/chapter-4/Resource-4.1-Leaf-Texture.jpg, and drop it in the 3D Viewport. It will be dropped as an image plane.

2. Press *N* to get the **Transform** panel on the right side.

3. Set the **Location** and **Rotation** of **X**, **Y**, and **Z** axes to 0 to have the plane laid down on the Blender grid.

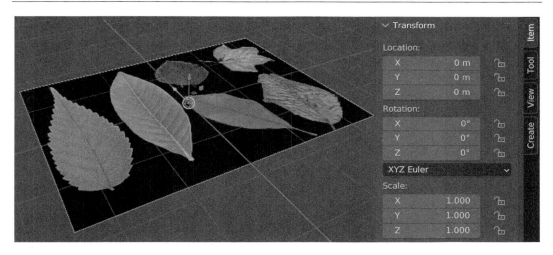

Figure 4.5 – Leaves reference

Creating a green leaf

Now, let's create the green leaf:

1. Press *7* on the numpad to switch to the top view.
2. Create a plane and place it on top of the leaf.

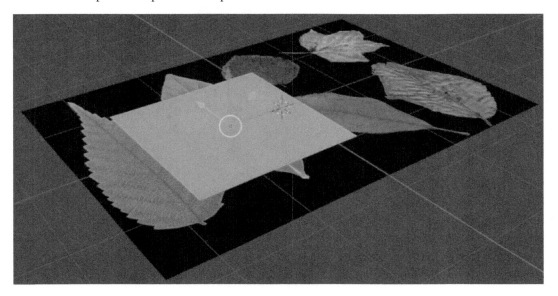

Figure 4.6– Adding a plane and putting it on top of the leaves reference

3.   Select the plane, jump into **Edit** mode, and insert five edge loops using *Ctrl + R*.

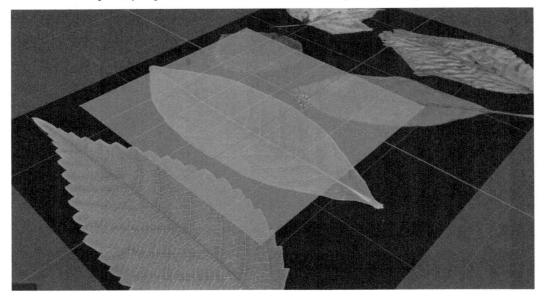

Figure 4.7– Inserting five edge loops in the plane

4.   Press *7* to go to the top view, then make the plane vertices fit the shape of the leaf reference:

Figure 4.8 –Aligning the plane with the leaf reference

5.   To create the middle vein of the leaf, add three vertical edge loops to the plane using *Ctrl + R*:

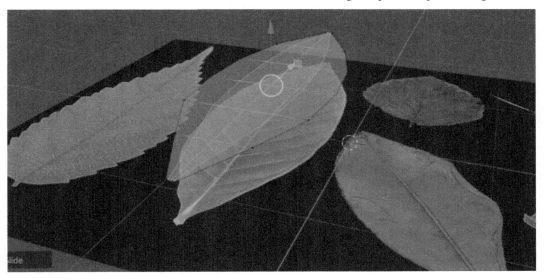

Figure 4.9 –Inserting three edge loops inside the plane

6.   Select the vertices shown in the following screenshot and move them up, and we get the shape of a leaf:

Figure 4.10 –Selecting middle plane vertices

7. Select the vertices shown in the following screenshot and move them up, and we get the shape of another leaf:

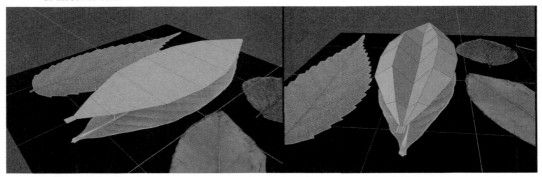

Figure 4.11 – Forming the shape of a leaf

Let's rotate the leaf using the **Proportional Editing** tool we used earlier with the ground to get a perfect result.

We'll select the last point of the leaf and rotate it around the X axis.

The rotation angle I used here is 40 degrees. This is the result:

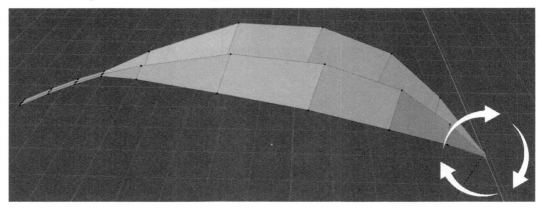

Figure 4.12 – Bending the leaf shape using the Proportional Editing tool

This way of spinning our leaf using the **Proportional Editing** tool gets us a perfect and organic leaf shape. Doing it manually will take time and won't be precise. Now let's add more details to our leaf.

Applying a Subdivision modifier to the leaf

The leaf still doesn't look good because it has a very small number of vertices. We need to add the Subdivision modifier to make it look smoother and more realistic. Let's look at the steps to do just that:

1. Select the leaf.

2. Jump into the modifier library represented by the wrench icon.

3. Click on **Add Modifier** and choose **Subdivision Surface**:

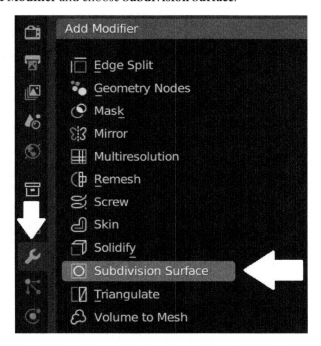

Figure 4.13 – Adding the Subdivision Surface modifier

The Subdivision Surface modifier is used to split the faces of a mesh into smaller faces, giving it a smooth appearance. Be careful with this modifier because this modifier doubles exponentially the number of vertices in your object. Later, we'll be spawning plants hundreds of times, which will heavily affect the performance of Blender. So, I set the number of subdivisions to only 1 for both **Levels Viewport** and **Render**:

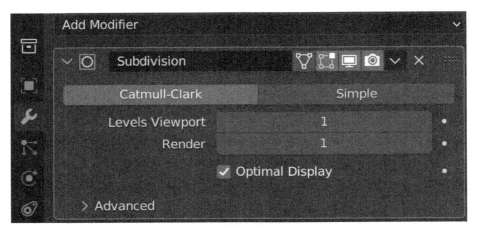

Figure 4.14 – Tweaking the Subdivision Surface modifier settings

4.   The last step is to shade smooth the surface of the leaf. So far, its edges look sharp. To do that, select the leaf, then right-click and choose **Shade Smooth**:

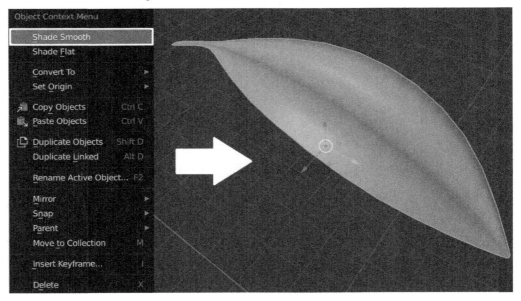

Figure 4.15 – Applying Shade Smooth to the leaf

We have finished creating the shape of the leaf, now let's texture it.

Texturing the leaf

Let's look at the steps to texture the leaf:

1. Select the leaf, go to **Material Properties**, and add a new material called `Leaf`.

2. Switch the bottom window to **Shader Editor**. You will find the **Principled BSDF** node related to the Leaf material we have created. Drag the Leaf texture we used before as a reference, drop it in the **Shader Editor**, and connect it to the **Base Color input**:

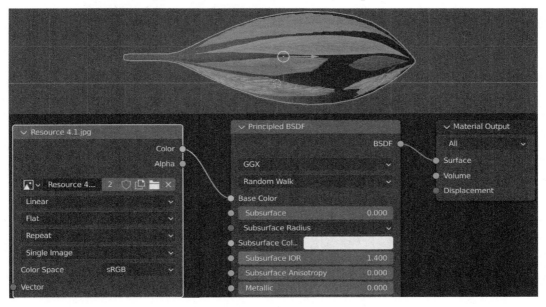

Figure 4.16 – Texturing the leaf

3. Our leaf doesn't look right so the next step, as you might guess, is to fix the UV map of the leaf. Switch the bottom window from **Shader Editor** to **UV Editor**.

4. Make sure that you're at the top of the leaf. Press *7* to switch to the top view.

5. Select the leaf and press *tab* to switch to **Edit** mode.

6. Press *U* and choose **Project from View**.

    Project from View is a mapping technique that takes the current view in the 3D view and unwraps the mesh as it appears. That's why you need to be at the top, to fully cover the leaf.

    After unwrapping, make sure to place the leaf vertices you have in the UV Editor on the green leaf image reference. Feel free to tweak the vertices to match the leaf texture.

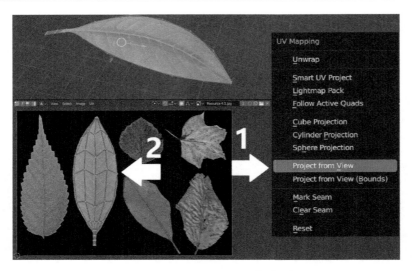

Figure 4.17 – Unwrapping the leaf

7. Next, we need to tweak the roughness and bumps of the leaf material, the same thing we did previously with materials such as wood and metal. This is the node setup of the leaf material:

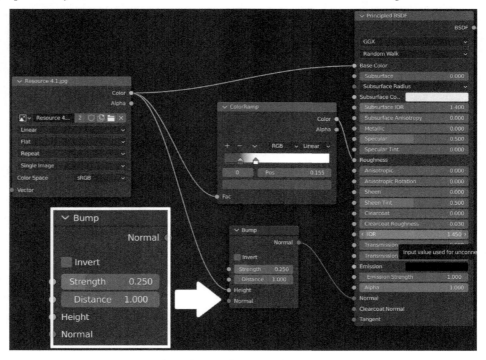

Figure 4.18 – Tweaking the roughness and bumps of the leaf material

This is what the leaf looks like after applying the roughness and bumps to it:

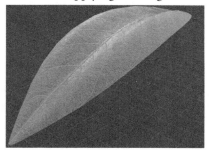

Figure 4.19 – Final result of the leaf

Let's create the stem of the plant; it has a cylindrical shape:

1. Create a cylinder mesh by pressing *Shift + A*.

2. Reduce the geometry of the cylinder to 8 vertices in the bottom-left tab in the 3D Viewport.

3. Set **Radius** to 0.004m (4 mm), and set **Depth** to 0.4m (40 cm).

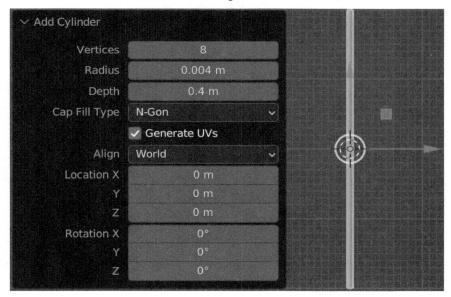

Figure 4.20 – Creating the stem of the plant

4. Select the cylinder, switch to Edit mode, and add edge loops vertically by pressing *Ctrl + R*. You can insert up to 5 edge loops. We need to keep our geometry low.

5. Scale down the top of the cylinder while enabling the **Proportional Editing** tool. In nature, stems get narrower toward the top. You need to scale down the top only on the *X* and *Y axes*. To do that, press *S + Shift + Z*. This way, you'll be excluding scaling on the *Z* axis.

6. Enable the **Proportional Editing** tool with **Sharp** mode applied to slightly move the top of the stem sideways. This will allow all the rest of the edge loops to follow smoothly.

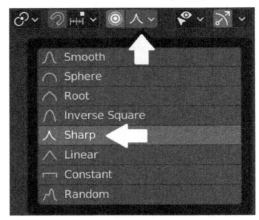

Figure 4.21 – Enabling the Sharp Proportional Editing tool

These are the three steps:

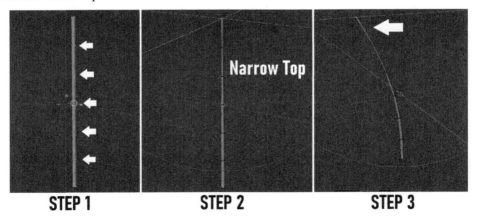

Figure 4.22 – Three steps to create a plant's stem

Now, let's connect the leaves to the stem:

1. For the base, duplicate the six leaves we created for the plant base and place them randomly at the bottom of the stem. They must be connected to the stem.

2. Add more layers of leaves as you go up.

3. With each level, scale down the size of the leaves:

Figure 4.23 – Connecting leaves to the stem

This is what the final shape of the plant looks like:

Figure 4.24 – Finishing the shape of the plant

Make sure to combine all the parts of the plant, leaves, and stem into a single object. To do that, select all the parts and press *Ctrl + J* to join them.

Creating the second type of plant

Let's use the same leaves reference to create the second green leaf. This one's shape is different. It has a wavy edge and it is longer than the previous one. We need that differentiation in shape between the two plants.

So, repeat the same steps we did with the previous leaf to create this new one. Feel free to make some changes to the shape as you like:

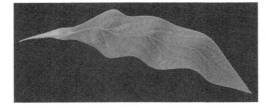

Figure 4.25 – Creating a different type of leaf

All leaves have the same center. Unlike the previous plant, this plant has no stem, so it will be easier to make. This is what the second plant looks like:

Figure 4.26 – Connecting the leaves to the center

We can create grass by scaling down on the X axis to make the leaf narrower, then expand it to make it look tall. Then we can use the **Proportional Editing** tool to make it look wavy:

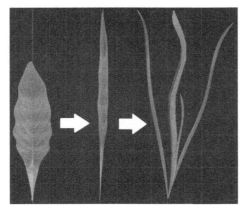

Figure 4.27 – Scaling down the leaf on the X axis

The last step is to create some dead leaves. Use the reference again and follow the same steps we did with other leaves to create these new dead leaves.

Creating the dry leaves

When modeling, make sure to keep the geometry as low as possible. These dead leaves will be small objects thrown on the ground:

Figure 4.28 – Creating dry leaves

Now that we have created plants and leaves, let's go ahead and texture our ground.

Texturing a realistic natural ground

Let's texture the ground using the forest texture available at this GitHub link: https://
github.com/PacktPublishing/3D-Environment-Design-with-Blender/
blob/5747aa3c8ad3808df62ac63c12f06db849113e3b/chapter-4/Resource-
4.2-Ground-Texture.jpg.

Here are the steps:

1. Select the plane.
2. Add new material.

3.   Drag and drop the ground texture and drop it in the **Shader Editor**.

4.   Connect it to the **Base Color input**.

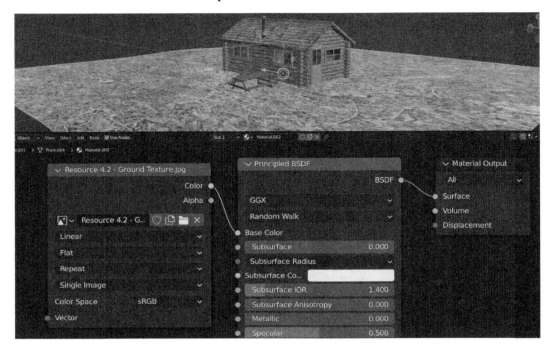

Figure 4.29 – Texturing the ground

5.   As you can see, the texture size is small. We need to scale it up. To do that, let's add **Mapping** and **Texture Coordinates** nodes and connect them to the **Ground Texture** node. I set the **X** and **Y** scale of the texture to 5.

6.   Add a **Bump** node with 0.250 strength and add a **ColorRamp** node to tweak the material's roughness. The node's setup should look like this:

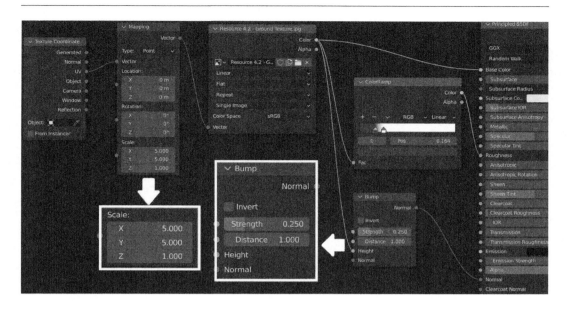

Figure 4.30 – Tweaking the ground material settings

Also, I would like to show you a cool trick to make the ground material look better. Let's search for the node called **Bright/Contrast** using *Shift + A* in **Shader Editor**.

7. Next, put it in between the ground texture and the **Base Color nodes**, and set the **Bright** value to -0.200:

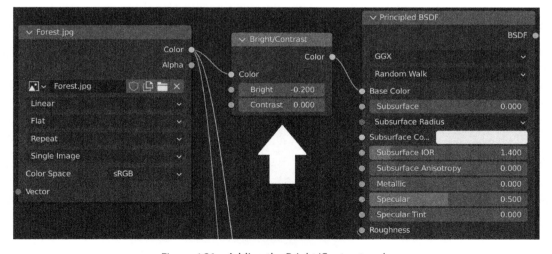

Figure 4.31 – Adding the Bright/Contrast node

=This is what the ground looks like before and after applying the brightness to it:

Figure 4.32 – The effect of the Bright/Contrast node applied to the ground

You can see that the colors look more vivid and fit the scene better.

Using a particle system to scatter plants and leaves in our scene

Now that we have plants and leaves, the next step is to scatter them all over the ground. You can do it manually by duplicating plants, scaling and spinning them around to make them look different, but this method will take a lot of time and effort and won't be efficient.

Luckily, there is a better way: using the particle system in Blender. It's used to scatter objects across a surface. In our example, we'll be scattering plants and leaves:

1. Select the ground, which is the object that will emit the particles.
2. Go to **Particle Properties**.
3. Press the plus icon to add a new particle system:

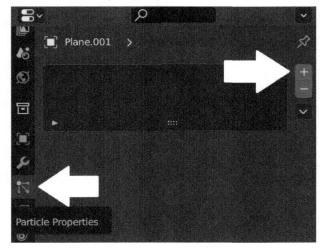

Figure 4.33 – Adding a new particle system to the ground

Immediately, you will see little spheres scattered all over the ground, as shown in *Figure 4.29*. This is the Emitter particle type.

Emitter particles are free particles that can be affected by force fields. Gravity will drag them down and wind will blow and push them away. This type of particle can be used to emit metal sparks.

In our example, we need particles that should be attached to the ground and have a hairy shape. That's why we'll be using the second type of particle, called **Hair**.

Figure 4.34 – Switching the particle system type from Emitter to Hair

So, switch the particle type from **Emitter** to **Hair** and check the **Advanced** checkbox.

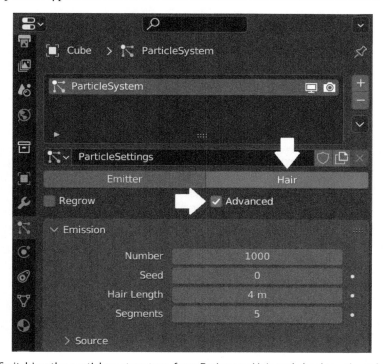

Figure 4.35 – Switching the particle system type from Emitter to Hair and checking the Advanced option

Now we need to replace the hair particles with the plant objects we created. To do that, follow these steps:

1. Inside **Particle Properties**, scroll down to the **Render** tab.

2. Change **Render As** from **Path** to **Object**.

3. Next, you will see an **Object** tab and, below it, you will find **Instance Object**. This is where we choose the object that will replace the hair particles.

4. Click on **Instance Object** and select the plant object we created:

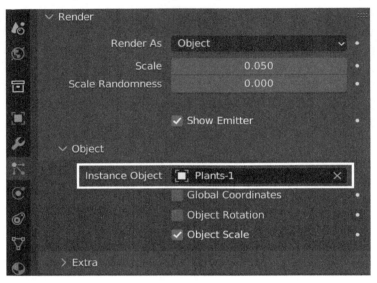

Figure 4.36 – Using the Plants-1 object as an Instance Object

Now, you will see that the hair particles are replaced with plants that are scattered all around the ground.

Figure 4.37 – Scattering plants in our wood cabin scene

We have to tweak the particle settings, starting with the orientation of the plants. At the moment, they look as if they've been laid down on the ground. We need to have them standing straight. Follow these steps to do that:

1. Go back to **Particle Properties** and find the **Rotation** tab. Check the little box to access the rotation settings.

2. The first setting to change is **Orientation Axis**. Change it from **Velocity/Hair** to **Global Y**.

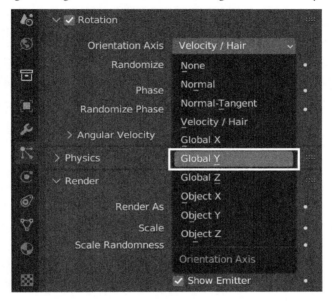

Figure 4.38 – Switching Orientation Axis to Global Y

3. Now, the plants should be standing upright, like in the following screenshot. If not, try another axis, such as **Global X** or **Global Z**:

Figure 4.39 – Change plant orientation from horizontal to vertical

4. Next, we need to fix the scale of the plants. To do that, go to the **Render** tab. You will find the **Scale** value. Replace it with a smaller value until the plant size seems reasonable. In my case, 0.01 works fine:

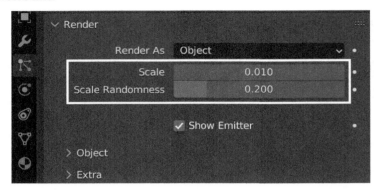

Figure 4.40 –Tweaking the Particles Scale and Scale Randomness values

5. The next setting is the **Scale Randomness**. This is a great setting that adds to the realism because as you know in nature it's almost impossible to have two objects that are exactly the same size. In Blender, by default, **Scale Randomness** is set to **0**, meaning that the scale of plants is the same.

Scale Randomness allows the plants to have random sizes. Set **Scale Randomness** to a lower value, such as 0.25, and this is the result:

Figure 4.41 –Randomizing the scale of plants particles in the wood cabin scene

You might notice that all the plants have the same rotation. We need to randomize the rotation of the plants:

1. Go to the **Rotation** tab.

2. Below the **Orientation Axis**, you will find the **Randomize** tab. Set it to a small value, such as 0.100:

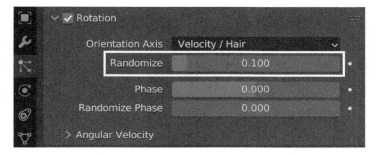

Figure 4.42 – Setting the Randomize value to 0.1

You can see the difference that randomizing the rotation makes to the plants:

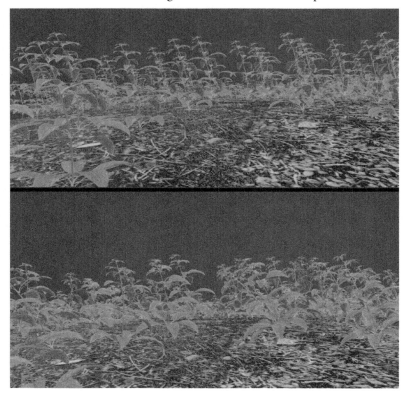

Figure 4.43 – Randomizing the plants particles

If you want to increase or decrease the number of plants, you can scroll up to the **Emission** tab and change the **Number** value. Keep in mind that this number heavily affects performance, and a higher number might cause your setup to start lagging:

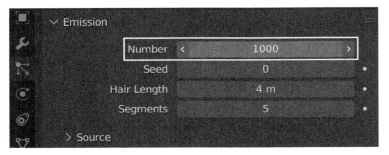

Figure 4.44 – Setting the particles number to 1000

Adding the second type of plants

Now that we have added the first plant type, let's add the second one:

1. The process is simple. We will create a new particle system:

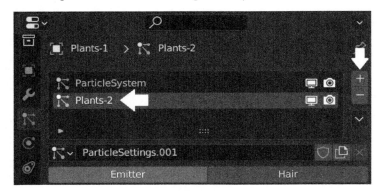

Figure 4.45 – Adding a new particle system for the second type of plants

2. And as we did in *Figure 4.36*, let's replace the **Instance Object** with the other types of plant. Make sure to create a new particle system for each plant and leaf and tweak the settings until you achieve a well-balanced natural scene.

3. The final step is to add the tree and bench assets that you will find in the resources to download, available at `https://github.com/PacktPublishing/3D-Environment-Design-with-Blender/blob/main/chapter-4/Wood%20Cabin%20Resources.zip`. Apply the Append method we used in *Chapter 3, Efficient Unwrapping and Texturing in Blender Figure 3.1.*

Figure 4.46 – Rendering the wood cabin scene in the 3D Viewport

Summary

In part one of this chapter, we created a realistic ground under our wood cabin and we learned how to use the **Proportional Editing** tool to add nice undulation to the ground. Then, we went through the process of creating, unwrapping, and texturing different types of plants and leaves.

Next, we learned how to use the particle system to scatter objects on a surface. In this case, we scattered plants and leaves all over the ground. We learned how to tweak the particle system settings, such as randomizing the scale and rotation of plants and controlling their quantity.

In this chapter, you've learned how to create a realistic natural scene with various plants and leaves in Blender. You've also learned how to model, texture, and place different types of plants in your environment. You've seen how to use the particle system in Blender to generate random plants in your scene.

In the next chapter, we will learn how to get better lighting in Blender. We will look at three different ways to apply realistic lighting to our wood cabin.

5

Achieve Photorealistic Lighting in Your Environment with Blender

Lighting can make or break any 3D project. In this chapter, we will explore the basics of lighting in Blender. We will look at three different ways to apply realistic lighting to our wood cabin scene, the different properties those three lighting methods offer, and how we can configure them.

The objective of this chapter is to achieve realistic lighting in our wood cabin scene that matches the color, direction, and intensity seen in the wood cabin reference image we're using.

First, we will break down the three Blender rendering engines to understand the difference between them and the role each one plays in achieving photorealism.

Then, we will learn how to use the sun to emit realistic lighting based on the Kelvin temperature scale, add a background to our scene, and then render it. We will also make use of the Blender **Sky Texture** node to light our environment, and finally we'll show how to achieve realistic lighting using HDRI maps.

In this chapter, we'll be covering the following topics:

- Differences between the three render engines of Blender
- Using the sun to emit realistic lighting
- Using a Blender Sky Texture node to light our environment
- Lighting our wood cabin with lamp objects

Technical requirements

This chapter requires a Mac or PC capable of running Blender Version 3.0 or above.

You can download the resources for this chapter from GitHub at `https://github.com/PacktPublishing/3D-Environment-Design-with-Blender/tree/main/chapter-5`

Differences between the three render engines of Blender

We will need to render our scene some point. Rendering is the process of turning a 3D scene into a 2D image. Blender includes three rendering engines that you can use; each one has its own strengths and weaknesses:

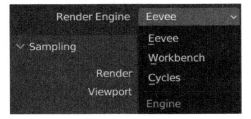

Figure 5.1 – Blender rendering engines

The Eevee render engine

Eevee is a real-time renderer; it uses some clever speedy tricks to render your scene really fast, but it sacrifices some aspects of realism. You should use this engine when realism is not the priority.

The Workbench render engine

The Workbench render engine is a modeling preview rendering engine optimized for fast rendering. This engine renders images similar to the Solid mode of the 3D Viewport. It is not intended for rendering final images. Personally, I use this engine when making animations as it helps you render the animation much faster in Solid mode. This allows you to check the flow of your animation without spending hours rendering it in the Cycles engine.

The Cycles render engine

Cycles works by tracing light rays from each pixel of a designated camera onto a scene; these rays are then reflected and absorbed by objects until they hit a light source or reach their bounce limit that you can define in **Light Paths**. Cycles uses multiple rays or samples from a pixel and slowly calculates the result. In terms of accuracy, it's the closest you can get to true photorealism. However, rendering using this process is very time consuming.

Cycles is a ray-tracing engine, meaning that when rendering a scene, Blender sends rays from the camera and when a ray hits a reflective surface, it repeats the process until it reaches a light source. It computes many different effects including shadows, mirrors, glossy reflections, and refractions. A downside to path tracing is noise. However, noise vanishes as more paths accumulate, which is why we need to check the **Denoise** box when using Cycles.

We'll be using the Cycles render engine heavily in our project.

Next, let's take a look at the first method we'll be following to add lighting to our scene.

Using the sun to emit realistic lighting

The first method we'll be using to add lighting to our scene is to create a sun light source. So, let's add it using the following steps:

1.   In our 3D Viewport, press *Shift + A*.

2.   Go to the **Light** tab and choose **Sun**:

Figure 5.2 – Adding a sunlight to the scene

Note

Make sure you're on the Cycles rendering engine, although this lighting method works well on both engines, Eevee and Cycle.

---

3.   Now, let's go ahead and switch the shading mode to **Rendered** in order to see how the lighting looks:

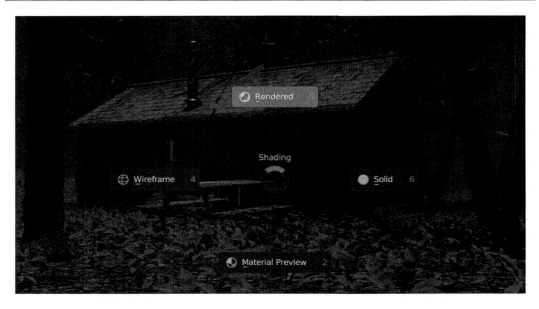

Figure 5.3 – Switching to Rendered view

4. The lighting currently looks dark and creepy so the first setting we need to adjust is the sun light's strength.

5. While selecting the sun object, jump into the **Object Data Properties** pane represented by the light bulb icon and find **Strength** value set to **1** by default. Increase it by ten times to 10:

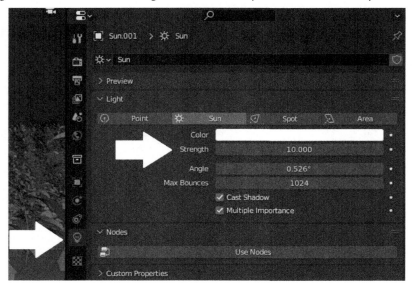

Figure 5.4 – Adjusting the strength of the sun light

6. Now, let's switch the shading mode one more time to **Rendered** to see the lighting effect of increasing the sun strength ten times:

Figure 5.5 – Switching to Rendered view

We're getting better. Now we need to adjust the rotation of the sun to make it match the lighting in our wood cabin reference image.

7. Select the **Sun** object and press *N* to access the **Transform** panel.

8. Change the **Rotation** on the **Y** axis to -30.

9. Set the **Z** axis rotation to 50.

Check the rendered mode again to see this:

Figure 5.6 – Rotating the sun object on the Y and Z axis

But here we can see that the shadow cast onto the cabin is too strong. We need to fade it a bit to match the same lighting as in our wood cabin reference.

To do that, select **Sun** object from the 3D Viewport and in the **Object Data Properties** pane, increase the **Angle** to a higher number. 60 degrees will be fine. This will reduce the strength of the shadow around our wood cabin:

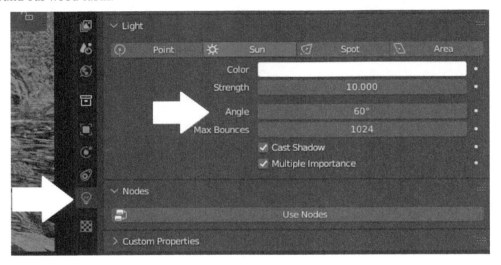

Figure 5.7 – Tweaking the sun shadow angle

This is how the lighting looks now:

Figure 5.8 – Rendering the scene on the 3D Viewport

Now the lighting looks better and is starting to resemble our reference, but it's still not 100% accurate. The reason it's not accurate is because of the sunlight color. The default color setting for sun lights is white, which is unrealistic, as you know when the sun rays pass through the earth's atmosphere, they look yellowish. So, let's change it to a warmer color:

Figure 5.9 – Changing the sun light color manually

As you can see, we can tweak the sun color, but this is not the right method of coloring the sun. You can change the sun light color manually, but you will never make it as accurate as real life. To fix this let me introduce to you the Kelvin scale.

The Kelvin scale

The Kelvin scale is a series of temperature units that can be used to create realistic natural lighting emissions in our scene. As you can see in the following diagram, if we set the Kelvin value for our sun to **5500**, it will emit daylight:

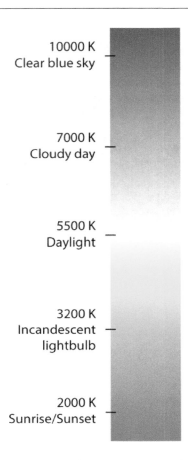

Figure 5.10 – Kelvin temperature scale

But how can we use this scale with our sun? This is where the **Blackbody** node comes to play.

Applying the Kelvin temperature scale to the sun using the Blackbody node

The **Blackbody** node converts the Kelvin temperature value to an RGB value. We apply it to our sun by doing the following:

1. Select the **Sun** object and jump into the **Object Data Properties** pane.

2. Click on **Use Nodes**:

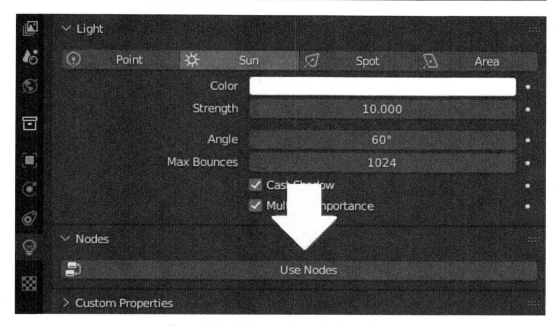

Figure 5.11 – Adding nodes to the Sun object

3.   The **Nodes** tab will appear. Next to the **Color** setting you will see a small yellow dot – click on it:

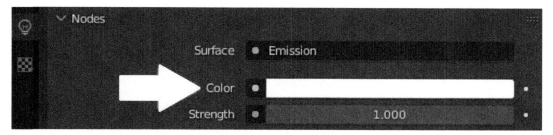

Figure 5.12 – Tweaking the color nodes of the Sun object

4.   Now you have access to a large menu. You will find the **Blackbody** node on the right side of the menu. Click on it and it will be added to our **Sun** object:

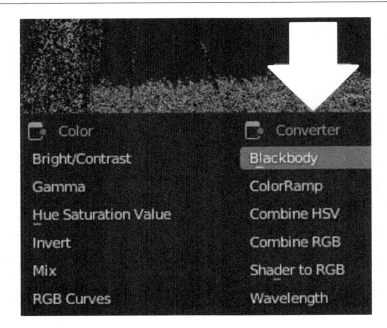

Figure 5.13 – Adding a Blackbody node to the Sun object

5. Now you will see the **Temperature** setting. This is where we will use the Kelvin scale. Based on our reference image, I would go with 5500 K, which is the daylight temperature:

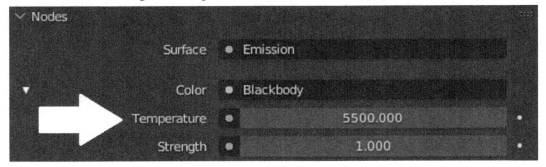

Figure 5.14 – Tweaking the Blackbody Temperature value of the sun object

6. If you now jump into **Rendered** mode, you should have perfect realistic lighting:

Figure 5.15 – Rendering the scene with the Blackbody node applied to the Sun object

Now that we have the lighting right, we need to fill the background of our rendered scene. The next step is to work on the background, which we will do in compositing mode, but before that we need to render our scene. For this, we will be using the Cycles render engine; we'll be using this heavily in our project.

Rendering our scene

Before rendering our scene we need to check some rendering settings. So, jump into the **Render Properties** tab represented by a camera icon and follow these steps:

1. To achieve maximum photorealism, we need first to opt for the **Cycles** render engine. Light behaves more realistically with this engine.

2. On the **Render** tab shown in the following screenshot, you will find **Max Samples** setting.

    Samples are the noisy boxes that appear as your scene is rendering. The more samples, the clearer your render is, but the longer it takes. In our case, we're still experimenting with the lighting, so we'll go with 64 samples to allow the rendering to process quickly. Once we're satisfied with the lighting, we can increase the samples to a higher number, between 200 and 500. Keep in mind that a higher number of samples is generally better, but there comes a point where more samples do almost nothing to your render – I'm talking about higher numbers, such as 10,000 samples.

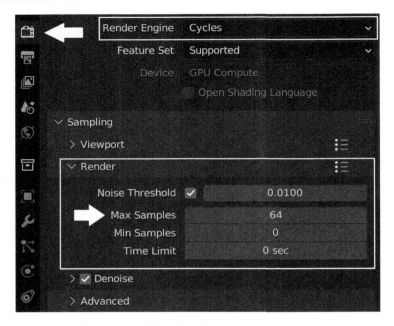

Figure 5.16 – Tweaking the rendering settings

3.   Also, since we want to add a custom background to our render to fill the dark areas in the back, we need to make our render transparent. To do that, let's check the **Transparent** box under the **Film** dropdown:

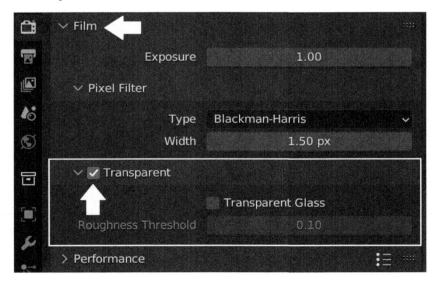

Figure 5.17 – Configuring the Transparent feature in our render settings

4. Alright, now let's go ahead and render our scene. So, on the top bar, click on **Render** and choose **Render Image**. The shortcut key is *F12*:

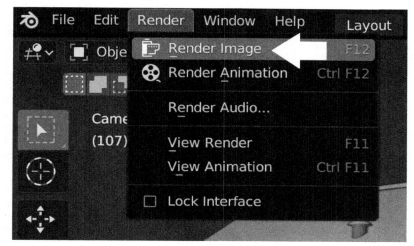

Figure 5.18 – Rendering the image

Now, let's see how we can add a background image to our render in the Compositing mode.

Adding a background to your render

Now the rendering process will begin. In the meantime, let's perform these steps:

1. Jump into the **Compositing** tab found on the top bar.

2. Check the **Use Node** box to access the compositing nodes. By default, you get two nodes, **Render Layers** and **Composite**.

3. Press *Shift + A* and search for the **Viewer** node.

4. Connect the **Render Layers Image** output to the **Image** input of the **Viewer** node. This way we'll be able to see the render result displayed on the **Compositing Node Tree** and any change we make to the render will be visible here:

Figure 5.19 – Switching to Compositing

This is the background that we'll be using:

Figure 5.20 – Reference of the background used to fill the transparent areas in our render

It's a nature scene that fits our wood cabin reference. You can find the image at the following GitHub link: https://github.com/PacktPublishing/3D-Environment-Design-with-Blender/blob/main/chapter-5/Nature-Background.jpg.

You can drag and drop the image file onto the **Composite** node setup. This will create a **Single Image** node:

Figure 5.21 – The Single Image node in Compositing

Now let's connect it to the node setup. To do that we will need an **Alpha Over** node. Search for it by pressing *Shift + A*. Basically, this **Alpha Over** node will fill the alpha space in our render. Connect it with the **Background** node **Image** output as follows:

Figure 5.22 – Mixing the nature background with the render using an Alpha Over node

The **Alpha Over** node has two **Image** inputs on the left side:

5. Connect the **Background Image** node to the top-left input of the **Alpha Over**, and the **Render Layers** node to the bottom **Image** input.

6. Connect the **Alpha Over** right-hand **Image** output to both the **Composite** and **Viewer** nodes' **Image** inputs.

Now we have the background image replacing the alpha space in our render, but the scale of the background image is not right. To fix that we will need a new node called **Scale**. Search for it using *Ctrl + A* and add it to the Compositing node setup.

This node should be placed between the **Background** image and **Alpha Over** nodes. Make sure to set it to **Render Size**, which will make the background image fit perfectly to the size of our render:

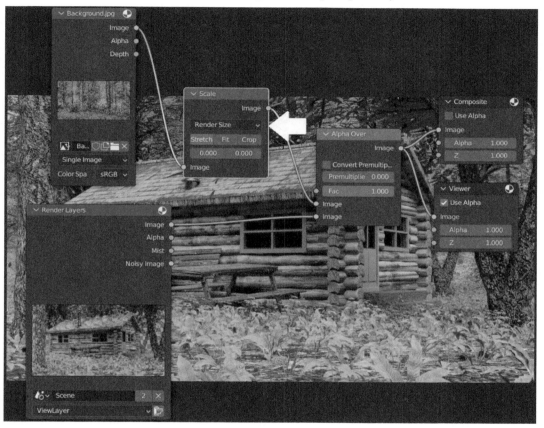

Figure 5.23 – Adjusting the scale of the background using a Scale node

You can see that the background perfectly fits the wood cabin. It looks like the background is part of the render.

Now that we've discussed the first lighting method using our sun, let's discover the second method of lighting: using a Blender Sky Texture node.

Using a Blender Sky Texture node to light our environment

The Sky Texture or Sky Box is a node provided by Blender that adds procedural sky lighting to our scene. To set it up, let's perform these actions:

1. Go to the **World Properties** panel, represented by a globe icon.

2. Click on the yellow dot next to **Color**.

3. Choose **Sky Texture** from the **Texture** list:

Figure 5.24 – Adding a Sky Texture to apply lighting to our environment

4. Turn off the **Transparent** feature in the **Render Properties** that we enabled earlier.

Now if you jump into the **Rendered** mode, you will see some nice lighting with a beautiful blue sky in the background:

Figure 5.25 – Rendering our scene by using a Sky Texture node as a light source

Keep in mind that the Sky Texture comes with its own sun, so if you already have a sun light in the scene just delete it.

In order to tweak the Sky Texture lighting, let's jump into the **Shader Editor**. But in order to see the **Sky Texture** node we need to switch from **Object** to **World**, as shown in the following screenshot. Basically, in **Object** mode we tweak objects' materials but in **World** mode, we get the chance to tweak the overall lighting of our scene:

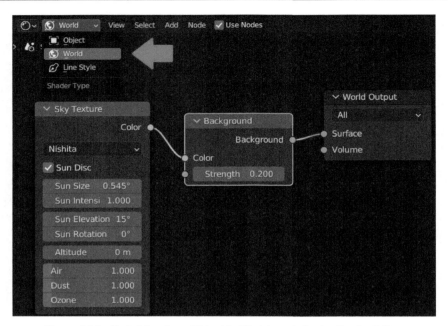

Figure 5.26 – Switching from Object to World mode in the Shader Editor

The **Sky Texture** will be connected to a **Background** node. This node is used to add background light emission and also helps us to control the brightness of our environment. If the lighting in your scene is too bright, you can reduce it to a value of 0.2 just like in our example.

Let's look at the values we need to adjust:

- **Sun Size**: If you increase the angle, the sun's diameter will get bigger:

Figure 5.27 – Tweaking the size of the sun

- **Sun Intensity** controls how intensely the sun will emit light.

- **Sun Elevation** changes the location of the sun. 0 degrees will put the sun on the horizon just like the sunset, while 90 degrees will position the sun vertically in the sky, just like in the middle of the day:

Figure 5.28 – Changing the location of the sun in the sky

The other settings are as follows:

- **Altitude** is the distance from the sea level to the location of the camera. 0 meters means that you will get the lighting at sea level. Increasing this value to something like 30000 meters will give you the lighting you see when you see a satellite.

Figure 5.29 – Sky Texture with Altitude set to 30000 m

- **Air** controls the density of air molecules.

- **Dust** controls the density of dust and water droplets.

- **Ozone** controls the density of ozone molecules and is used to make the sky appear bluer.

Now, we will experiment with another way of lighting our wood cabin by using lamp objects.

Lighting our wood cabin with lamp objects

I've also added some lamps around the wood cabin. To add light points in your scene, use the following steps:

1. Press *Shift + A*, go to the **Light** tab and choose **Point**.

2. Create multiple **Points** and place them around the wood cabin where you might hang lamps in real life:

Figure 5.30 – Adding lamp objects to the scene

Next, we need to adjust the color of the point light. To do that we'll repeat the same process we did with the sun previously:

1. Select the **Point** object.

2. Jump into the **Object Data Properties** pane and click on **Use Nodes**.

3. Add the **Blackbody** node and set its **Temperature** to 2.500.

Based on the Kelvin scale, we will get a warm lighting color similar to an incandescent light source, which fits perfectly the wood cabin theme:

Figure 5.31 – Rendering the scene while applying the Blackbody node to the lamps

Now that we've learned how to use the **Sky Texture** node along with point lights to apply lighting to our scene, let's examine the final method to apply realistic lighting to our scene: using HDRI maps.

Setting up realistic lighting using HDRI maps

HDRI stands for **high dynamic range image**. Think of this as a large image that covers 360 degrees of the surroundings. They are created by combining several pictures of the same scene.

When we assign an HDRI map to our environment, Blender will wrap it around an invisible sphere that will surround our 3D scene from all angles:

Figure 5.32 – Demonstration of how Blender deals with HDRI maps

An environment light surrounds all of the objects in your 3D scene and will light and reflect off all surfaces. This makes HDRI maps very powerful for environment lighting.

How to set up an HDRI environment background for our scene

In order to set up the HDRI map, let's switch the **Shader Editor** from **Object** mode to **World** mode, just as we did earlier in *Figure 5.26*.

Next, in the **Shader Editor**, press *Shift + A* and search for **Environment Texture**. Connect its **Color** output to the **Color** input of **Background**:

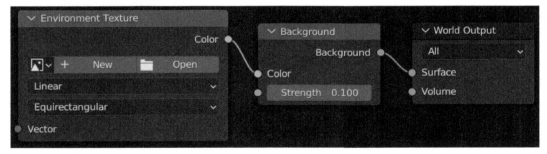

Figure 5.33 – Adding an Environment Texture node in the Shader Editor

Now let's download the HDRI map; you will find it in this GitHub link `https://github.com/PacktPublishing/3D-Environment-Design-with-Blender/blob/main/chapter-5/Nature%20HDRI%20Map.exr` under the name of Nature HDRI Map.exr.

Once you download the HDRI map, click on **Open** on the **Environment Texture** node and choose it from there.

> **Note**
> Make sure to adjust the **Background** node's **Strength** to 1 to get the default lighting of the HDRI map.

Now, straight out of the box we have realistic lighting projected in our scene. In order to tweak the **Environment Texture** node, we will need two additional nodes: **Mapping** and **Texture Coordinate**. Search for them and add them to the **Shader Editor**, then connect them as shown in the following screenshot:

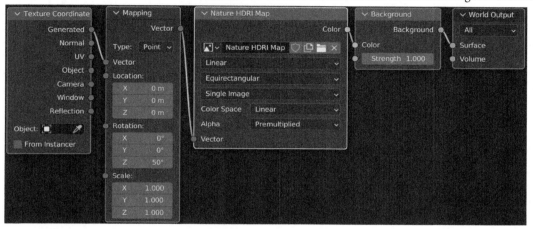

Figure 5.34 – Tweaking the HDRI map rotation by using the Mapping and Texture Coordinate nodes

Now, using the **Mapping** node, we can rotate the HDRI map around the scene to produce different lighting effects. In my case I set it to 50 degrees and rendered the scene. This is the result I got:

Figure 5.35 – Final render of the wood cabin scene

This is the wood cabin reference image we've been using:

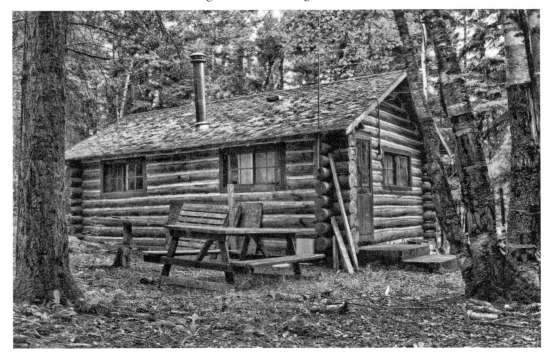

Figure 5.36 – Reference used to create the wood cabin scene

And there you have it. We finished our first objective, which is to turn our reference image into a realistic 3D scene in Blender. In the next chapter, we'll be expanding our environment by creating landscapes.

Summary

In this chapter, first, we broke down the differences between the Blender rendering engines, understanding the role each one plays in achieving photorealism. We then covered three ways to apply lighting to our wood cabin scene. We achieved our objective, which was to make our scene match the wood cabin reference image we're using. We explored the basics of lighting in Blender by taking a look at the different ways we can add light to a scene, the properties that those different light sources offer, and how we can configure them.

In the next chapter, we will zoom out and expand our environment. We will also learn to create large, natural, and realistic landscapes in Blender.

Part 2:
Creating Realistic Landscapes in Blender

This is the main topic of our book. We will learn how to generate realistic snow and rocky mountains. Then, we will create a nice-looking mud texture using procedural texturing and apply it to the landscape. We will also create realistic, natural-looking water and animate it in our landscape environment.

This part includes the following chapters:

- *Chapter 6, Creating Realistic Landscapes in Blender*
- *Chapter 7, Creating and Animating Realistic, Natural-Looking Water*
- *Chapter 8, Creating Procedural Mud Material*
- *Chapter 9, Texturing the Landscape with Mud Material*

6

Creating Realistic Landscapes in Blender

In this chapter, you will learn how to create realistic landscapes with snow and rock in Blender. Modeling landscapes by hand is a tedious process. This is when the **Another Noise Tool (A.N.T.)** Landscape add-on comes in handy. It can help us generate terrain for our scenes way quicker than it would be to model terrain by hand. This is an essential technique that will be a great addition to any 3D artist's arsenal.

In this chapter, we will cover the following topics:

- Enabling the A.N.T. Landscape add-on
- Creating landscapes using the A.N.T. Landscape add-on

Technical requirements

This chapter requires a Mac or PC capable of running Blender Version 3.0 or above.

You can download the resources for this chapter from GitHub at `https://github.com/PacktPublishing/3D-Environment-Design-with-Blender/tree/main/chapter-6`

Enabling the A.N.T. landscapes add-on

A.N.T. uses different procedural noises to generate various landscapes. The first thing is to enable it. Let's jump into a brand-new scene and do the following:

1. Click on **Edit** on the top bar and choose **Preferences…**:

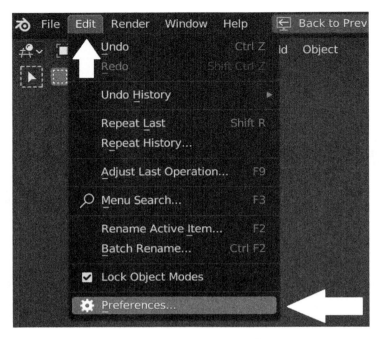

Figure 6.1 – Accessing Blender Preferences

2. Select **Add-ons** and type `landscape` in the search bar. The list will filter the add-on and you can enable it by checking the checkbox to the left of the add-on name.

3. Simply check the box next to **Add Mesh: A.N.T Landscape**:

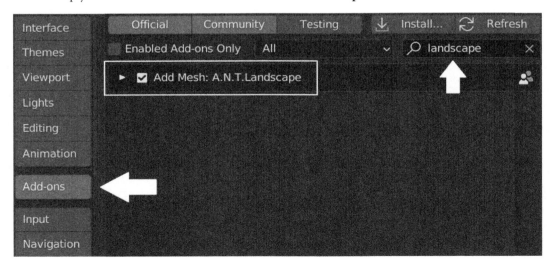

Figure 6.2 – Searching for the A.N.T Landscape add-on

And voila, you have successfully installed the add-on. To check whether it's installed properly, you can go back to the 3D Viewport, press *Shift + A*, go to **Mesh**, and you should see **Landscape** in the bottom list:

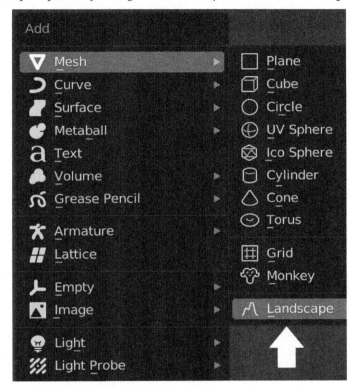

Figure 6.3 – Searching for a Landscape 3D object using Shift + A

Now that the add-on has been successfully installed, we can go ahead and use it in our scene.

Creating landscapes using the A.N.T add-on

To add landscapes, let's press *Shift + A*, choose **Mesh,** and on the bottom, you'll find **Landscape**; click on it and voila – you have a landscape in your scene:

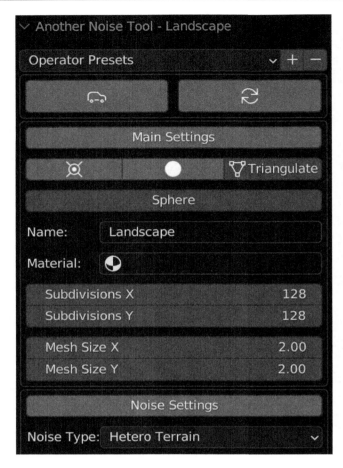

Figure 6.4 – Adding a Landscape 3D object

Adding a landscape using A.N.T. should open a menu on the left-hand side of the 3D Viewport – you can press *F9* to maximize it. We will use this menu to customize the landscape shape.

> **Note**
> Make sure not to click – otherwise, if you click away, you will lose your settings. Be careful to only click once you're satisfied with the shape of the landscape you're building.

Tweaking the shape of the landscape

Let's look at the steps to do this:

1. The first setting to change is **Mesh Size** to 5 . 00 on both the **X**- and **Y**-axes:

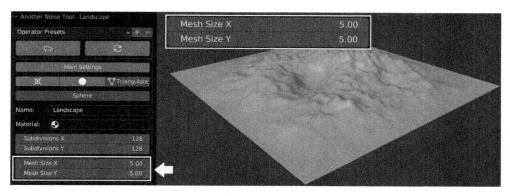

Figure 6.5 – Tweaking the landscape mesh size

2. Next, **Noise Type**: let's change it from the default, **Hetero Terrain**, to **Slick Rock**, and switch **Noise Basis** from the default, **Blender**, to **Voronoi F2**:

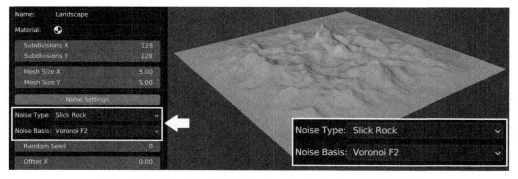

Figure 6.6 – Changing Noise Type for the landscape to Slick Rock

3. At the bottom, we will set **Falloff** to **Y** to make it continuous on the *x* axis and set the **Falloff Y** value to only **1.00**:

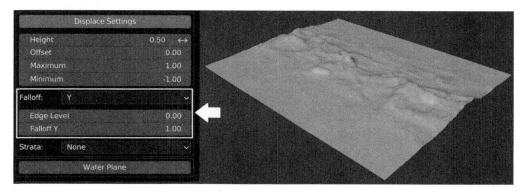

Figure 6.7 – Setting Falloff Y of the landscape to 1

4. Next, let's change **Size X** to **2.00** to expand the landscape and tweak the **Height** settings – we need to increase it from **0.50** to **0.75**, and change **Offset** to **0.10**:

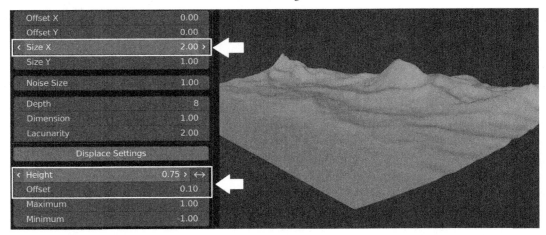

Figure 6.8 – Tweaking the size, height, and offset of the landscape

5. Finally, let's increase **Subdivisions X** and **Subdivisions Y** to **512** to get more detail in our landscape:

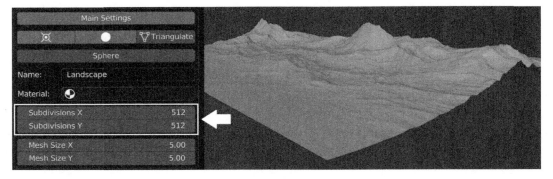

Figure 6.9 – Changing the landscape X and Y subdivisions

We have the shape of the landscape, but we need to make sure it has the right realistic scale.

Giving the landscape a real-scale measurement

Before scaling our landscape, we need to research to get the scale right. I found that the average landscapes rise at least 300 meters above the surrounding land, so anything in the 300 m height range should be believable.

Let's scale up our landscape:

1. Select the landscape object and switch to **Edit Mode**.
2. Press *N* to access the right panel where the object dimensions are displayed.
3. Scale the landscape by pressing *S* while keeping an eye on the **Z** dimension value:

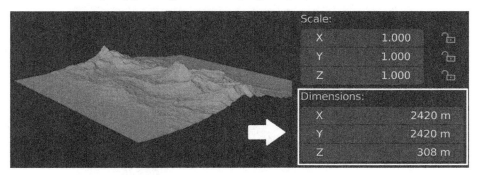

Figure 6.10 – Scaling up the landscape object to 308 meters in height

And there we go – we have an excellent start to a realistic landscape. The next step is to texture it.

Creating a realistic snowy mountain

Select the mountain object, jump into **Material Properties**, and create a new material called Mountain:

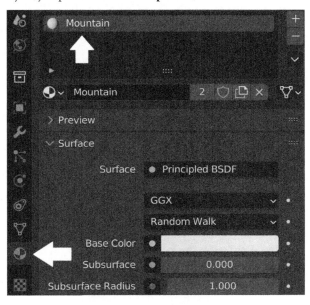

Figure 6.11 – Adding a material called Mountain

Switch the bottom window of Blender to the **Shader Editor** window and let's start tweaking the **Mountain** material:

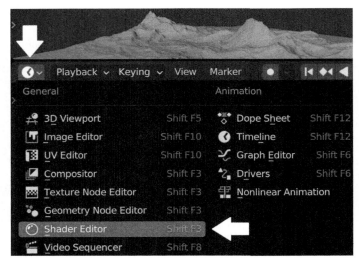

Figure 6.12 – Switching the bottom window to Shader Editor

Now, I want to create a snow mask, which is a black and white mask that will tell Blender what portions of the mountains we want to be rock and what portions of the mountain we want to be snow.

To explain further, we need to highlight only the flat surfaces that are facing the *z* axis in our landscape because these are the areas where the snow will gather.

To do that, let's add the following nodes.

Add a **Geometry** node:

Figure 6.13 – Adding a Geometry node

This node gives us geometric information about the object it's assigned to. In our case, the information we need here is **Normal**.

Let's first assign the **Normal** slot of the **Geometry** node to the **Color** slot of the **Principled BSDF** node:

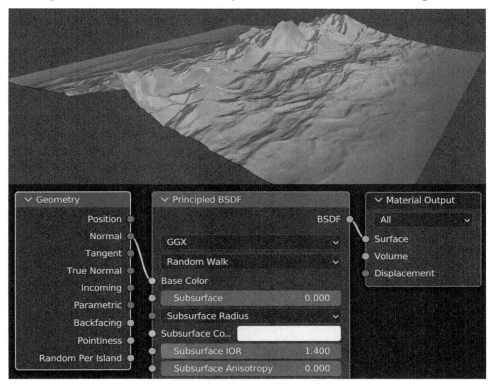

Figure 6.14 – Adding a Geometry node

This is how our landscape appears now:

Figure 6.15 – Displaying landscape with Normal Geometry

The **Normal** slot of the **Geometry** node is coloring our object in three colors: red, green, and blue. These RGB colors translate to *x*, *y*, and *z* coordinates:

- Surfaces that are aligned with the *y* axis will be green
- Flat surfaces will be blue
- Surfaces that are aligned with the *x* axis will be red

Since there is no 100% flat surface, we're not seeing 100% of the blue, green, or red colors.

In the cube example here, you can see the three colors displayed clearly because the faces of the cube are perfectly aligned with the *x*-, *y*-, and *z*-axes:

Figure 6.16 – Displaying Normal Geometry of a cube

Now, you might wonder how this normal *x*, *y*, and *z* stuff will be useful to us. Basically, this is where the **Separate XYZ** node comes into play.

Using the Separate XYZ node

The **Separate XYZ** node will allow us to separate the normal *x*-, *y*-, and *z*-colors and pick any axis we want: *x*, *y* or *z*:

- Let's add the **Separate XYZ** node to our node setup:

Figure 6.17 – Adding a Separate XYZ node

- Let's connect the **Normal** slot of the **Geometry** node to the **Vector** slot of **Separate XYZ**.

- On the right side of **Separate XYZ**, connect the **X** slot to **Base Color** on **Principled BSDF**:

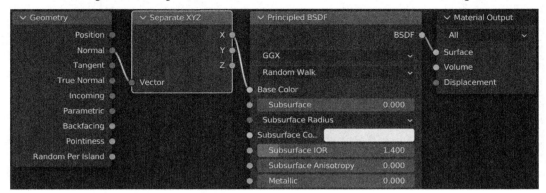

Figure 6.18 – Connecting the Geometry node to Separate XYZ, then to the Principles BSDF node

This way, we'll be only seeing the faces that are aligned with the red *x* axis.

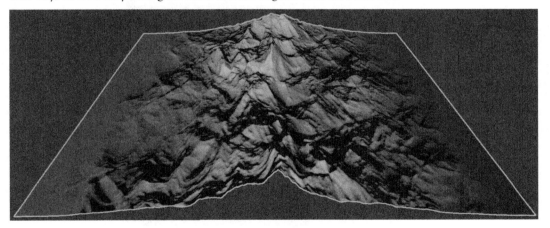

Figure 6.19 – Switching to Material Preview to check the landscape

I just want you to see this nice effect but actually, we're looking to highlight the top faces that are aligned with the *z* axis.

To have more control over the mask we're creating, we need to add a **ColorRamp** node and connect all three nodes as follows:

1. Move the white handle to the left until you see the **Pos** value set to 0.85

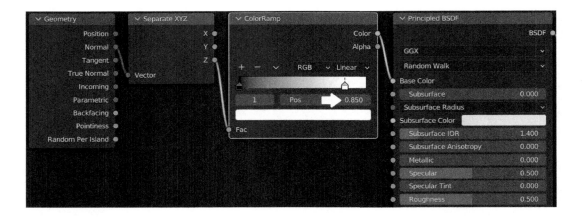

Figure 6.20 – Connecting the mask node setup to Base Color

2. Switch the **Interpolation** type of **ColorRamp** from **Linear** to **Constant**; this will make the black and white mask edges sharp:

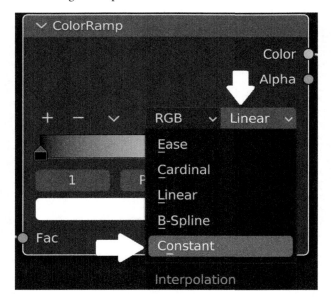

Figure 6.21 – Switching the ColorRamp type from Linear to Constant

This is what our landscape snow mask looks like:

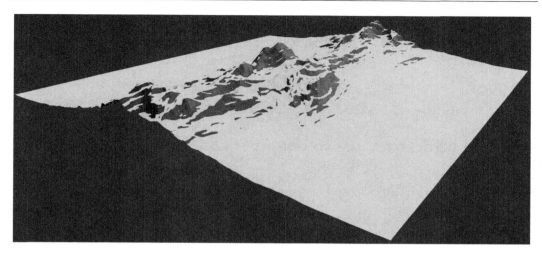

Figure 6.22 – Landscape in Material Preview with the mask node setup applied

When working with nodes, you might want to preview a particular node to see the effect it has on the whole material you're working on.

Using the node wrangler to display nodes

In order to preview any node, we can press *Ctrl + Shift* and left-click on the node we want to preview. But this shortcut won't work unless you enable the **Node Wrangler** add-on.

You can see how to enable the **Node Wrangler** add-on in the *The fastest way to set up PBR materials in Blender* section of *Chapter 10, Creating Natural Assets: Rock*.

For example, I pressed *Ctrl + Shift* and left-clicked on the **Geometry** node:

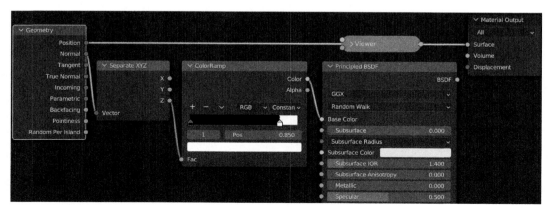

Figure 6.23 – Displaying the Geometry node using the Ctrl + Shift + left-click Node Wrangler shortcut

Blender will connect the node you want to preview to a **Viewer** node. The **Viewer** node is then connected directly to the **Material Output** node. This way, you will only see the **Geometry** node exactly as in *Figure 6.14*.

To preview the entire node setup, press *Ctrl + Shift* and left-click on **Principled BSDF**.

Now that we have the snow mask applied, the next step is to replace the black areas with rocks.

Adding the Rocks texture to our mountain

We'll be using the rock texture, which you can find at this GitHub link: https://github.com/PacktPublishing/3D-Environment-Design-with-Blender/blob/main/chapter-6/Rocks.jpg.

Drag and drop this rock image texture into **Shader Editor**:

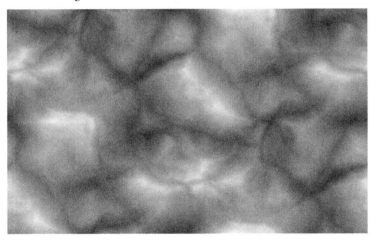

Figure 6.24 – Rock height map texture

We need to mix it with our mask:

1. Add a **MixRGB** node.
2. On the top **Fac** slot, connect the **Color** slot of the **ColorRamp** node.
3. On the **Color2** slot, connect the **Rocks image texture**.
4. Add **Displacement** Node.
5. Connect MixRGB Color slot to the **Displacement Height** slot then connect the Displacement node to the **Material Output Displacement** slot.
6. Increase the **Scale** value of the **Displacement** to 10

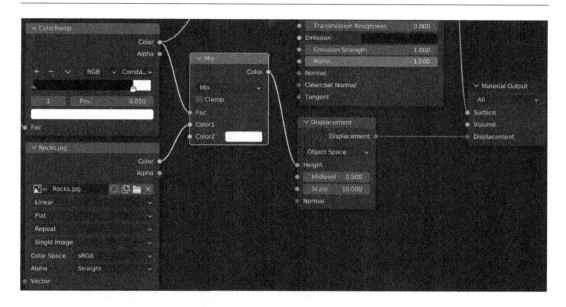

Figure 6.25 – Adding the Rock height map texture to the node setup

7. The last step to do is to scale up the rock image texture 10 times – to do that, let's add two additional nodes, **Mapping** and **Texture Coordinates**, and connect them as shown in *Figure 6.26*:

8. Make sure to scale up the **X** and **Y** values on the **Mapping** node to **10.000**:

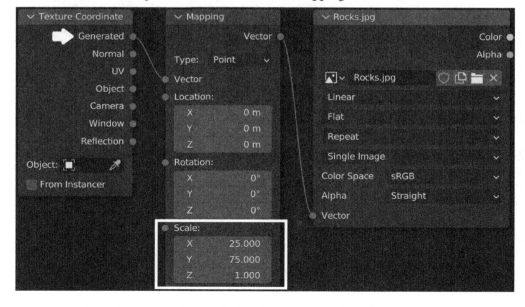

Figure 6.26 – Changing the Scale settings of the Rock height map texture

In order to see the mountain texture even better, let's set **Sky Texture**.

Adding Sky Texture to lighten our world

In **Shader Editor**, let's switch its type from **Object** to **World** – this way, we'll be able to adjust the lighting of our environment:

- Press *Shift + A* and search for Sky Texture.
- Connect it to the **Background** node:

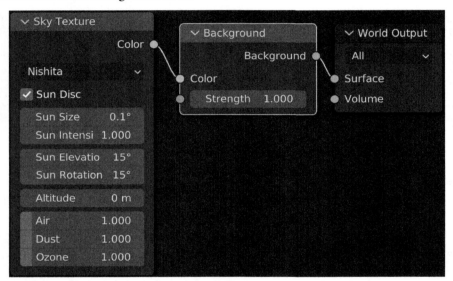

Figure 6.27 – Adding Sky Texture to lighten the scene

Now that we have decent lighting in our scene, let's do a quick render of our environment to see the landscape with the displacement map applied.

Rendering our mountain with the Displacement map applied

Now, if we jump back to the 3D Viewport and switch to the **Rendered** view, this is what our mountain will look like:

Figure 6.28 – Rendering the landscape on the 3D Viewport with the snow mask node setup applied

It has this nice effect of snow melting from the top to the bottom. It looks beautiful!

Changing the shape of the mountain

We're planning to add a river to our scene, and as you know, rivers are always at the bottom (water always reaches the bottom) of a mountain. Let's look at the steps to add the river:

1. Select the **Mountain** object.
2. Switch to **Edit Mode** by pressing *Tab*.
3. Press *7* to switch to the top view.
4. Press *Z* and switch to **Wireframe** (this way, our geometry will be transparent, and if we select a portion of our object, we won't miss any vertices).
5. Select either the right half or left half of the bridge, in our example we will select the left side:

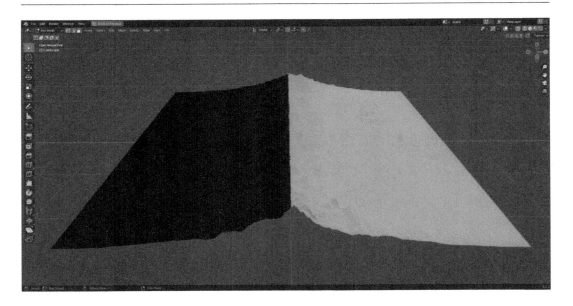

Figure 6.29 – Example showing the right half of the landscape selected on Edit Mode

It's black because it's heavy with details. We have around 262,000 vertices to work with on this mountain; the density of the vertices makes the entire mountain look black on **Wireframe**.

> **Quick tip**
>
> If you want to see the number of vertices you have in a particular object, you can click on **Show Overlay**, which you will find at the top right of the 3D Viewport, and enable **Statistics**.

Once you pick **Statistics** in **Show Overlay**, you will get access to the **Objects** and **Vertices** data:

- **Objects**: This shows the number of objects you are selecting.
- **Vertices**: The first number shows the number of vertices selected, and after the slash, you have the total number of vertices that the selected object has. The same thing goes for **Edges**, **Faces**, and **Triangles**:

Figure 6.30 – Enabling the Statistics feature

6. With the left side of the mountain selected, press *P* to separate it from the rest.

7. Press *Tab* to exit **Edit Mode**.

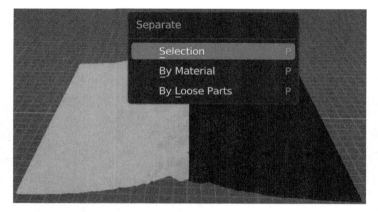

Figure 6.31 – Separating the half-selected part of the landscape

8. Move the separated part of the mountain to the right-hand side until both mountain parts match perfectly:

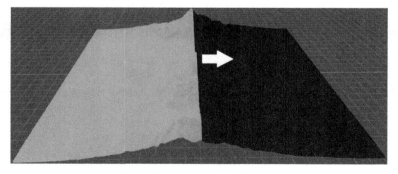

Figure 6.32 – Preparing the half-separated part of the landscape on the left side

9.   Move it to the right until it matches with the left:

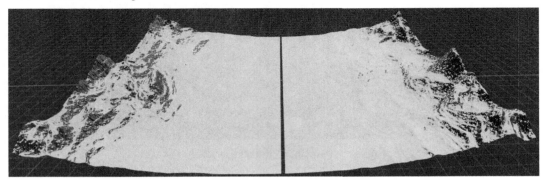

Figure 6.33 – Moving the half-separated part of the landscape to the right side

10. Now, we need to connect both parts of the mountain, so select both parts and press *Ctrl + J* to join both parts into a singular part.

11. Next, we need to fill the gap between these two parts. Select the mountain and switch to **Edit Mode**.

12. Zoom into the intersection part between the two sides of the mountain:

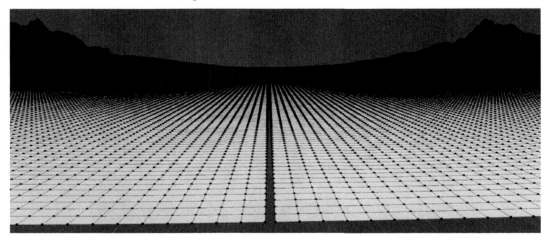

Figure 6.34 – Zooming into the intersection part between the two sides of the mountain

To fill the gap shown in *Figure 6.30*, we'll be using the **Bridge Edge Loops** feature. To do that, we need to select both mountain edges first.

13. Press *Alt* and left-click on the first side of the mountain.

14. Hold *Shift* to keep the first selection active.

15. Press *Alt* and left-click on the second side of the mountain.

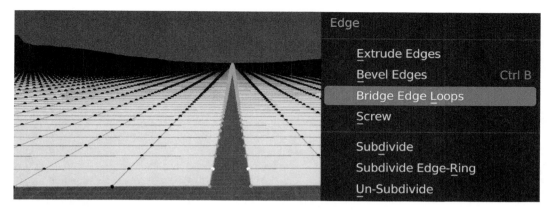

Figure 6.35 – Selecting both edges of the side parts of the mountain

16. Now, in order to fill that gap shown in *Figure 6.35*, you can press *Ctrl + E* and choose **Bridge Edge Loops**. This way, we will fill the gap between the two mountain parts and make it a single large beautiful mountain like this:

Figure 6.36 – Joining both landscape parts

17. Now, if we jump into **Object Mode** and press *Z* to switch to **Rendered**, we will have an excellent mountain curve that will be perfect for adding a river at the bottom:

Figure 6.37 – Rendered scene of the landscape

To demonstrate that, I've added a plane and put it at the lowest point of the mountain.

18. I've added a new material to the plane and changed its color to a sky-bluish color. I've also reduced **Roughness** to **0** in order to have a completely glossy and reflective river material:

Figure 6.38 – Adding a basic river to the landscape

The river looks fake right now, but don't worry about it – this is just a demonstration of where the river will be placed. In the next chapter, we'll be focusing on creating a photorealistic river that makes your scene stand out.

Summary

In this chapter, we went through the process of creating a realistic snow and rocky mountain. We started by installing the **A.N.T. Landscape** built-in add-on, and then added a landscape, tweaked its settings, and changed its shape to make it look as realistic as possible.

In *Part 2*, we focused on texturing the landscape by creating a snow and rock mask using procedural texturing.

In the next chapter, we will be bringing in our wood cabin and starting work on more details in our landscape – details such as a realistic river, stones, and rocks, and plants such as grass and flowers – and texturing the landscape differently.

7
Creating and Animating Realistic, Natural-Looking Water

Water is such a complex material with specific features such as reflection and refraction. In this chapter, we will take a look at creating an animated and realistic river from scratch.

We will learn how to use **Glass BSDF** and **Transparency BSDF** to achieve the kind of reflection and refraction that real water has. We will learn how to create and switch between shaders, and change the colors of shaders to achieve a nice-looking water surface.

Then, we will add a wave effect to the surface of the water using **Noise Texture**. Finally, we will learn how to animate the waves on the surface by inserting keyframes into the **Timeline** editor.

In this chapter, we'll be covering the following topics:

- Creating a realistic, natural river
- Animating the water flow

Technical requirements

This chapter requires a Mac or PC capable of running Blender Version 3.0 or above.

Creating a realistic, natural river

In the previous scene, we created a snow and rock landscape. Now, let's fill it with details – starting by adding a river to our scene.

Let's add a plane that's going to represent the water in our scene:

1. In the 3D Viewport, press *Shift + A* and create a plane object.

2. Scale the plane object by pressing *S* to make it fit the landscape size.

3. Move the plane object down until it collides perfectly with the bottom curve of the landscape. We just need to show a little bit of the plane on the surface. Take a look at *Figure 7.1* here, which shows where to place the plane object that we have created:

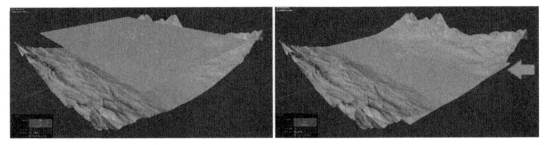

Figure 7.1 – Fitting the plane to the bottom curve of the landscape

Now that we have placed the plane object at the bottom of the landscape, we need to create a water material and assign it to this plane.

Creating a water material

Now that we have our plane, let's add a material called **Water** to it:

1. Select the plane object.

2. Go to **Material Properties**.

3. Add a material called **Water** to the plane object.

4. Switch the bottom menu of Blender to **Shader Editor** so that we can edit our material.

    Here are the preceding steps shown in our Blender scene:

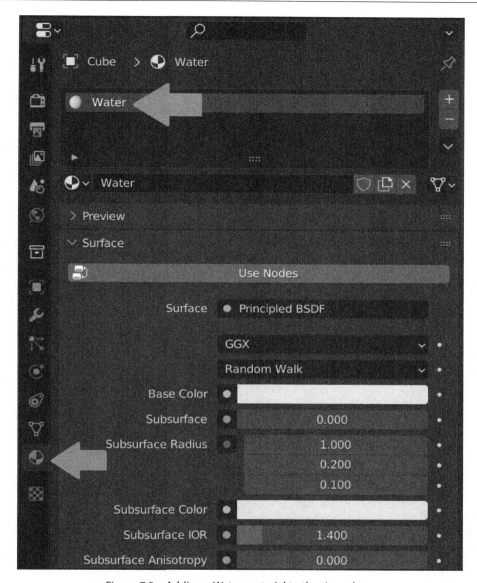

Figure 7.2 – Adding a Water material to the river plane

The first thing to do is to delete the **Principled BSDF** node; we don't need it to create our water material.

5. Select the **Principled BSDF** node, press *X*, and it will be deleted. We'll be left with the **Material Output** node alone:

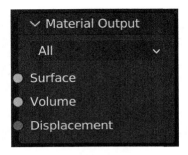

Figure 7.3 – The Material Output node

To create water, we will need to mix two effects: **reflectivity** and **transparency**.

6. Let's add a **Glass BSDF** node. Search for it by hitting *Shift + A* in **Shader Editor**. This node works like a glass shader. It is used for creating materials that refract and reflect light passing through them at certain angles.

    For transparency, we'll search for a node called **Transparent BSDF**. **Transparent BSDF** is used to add transparency without refraction, passing straight through the surface as if there were no geometry there.

    Figure 7.4 shows the **Glass BSDF** node, the **Transparent BSDF** node, and the **Material Output** node:

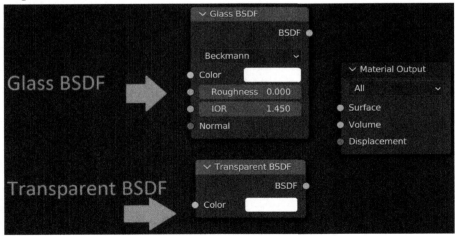

Figure 7.4 – Glass BSDF and Transparent BSDF

In **Glass BSDF**, we have a value called **IOR**, which stands for **Index of Refraction**. The IOR is a measure of how much a ray of light bends when passing from one medium to another. Each material has its own IOR (water, glass, plastic, and so on).

If you do a Google search on the IOR of water, you will find that it's equal to **1.33**:

About 10,400,000 results (0.50 seconds)

IOR water

Water has an IOR of **1.33**.

https://www.cineversity.com › wiki › Index_of_Refracti...   ⋮

Index of Refraction - IOR Wiki - Cineversity

Figure 7.5 – Search that shows the IOR for water

7.   Let's replace the IOR default value, **1.450**, with the IOR of water, 1.330.

Figure 7.6 – The Glass BSDF node

8.   The next step is to merge the transparency and the reflection; to do that, let's search for a node called **Mix Shader**.

Figure 7.7 – The Mix Shader node

The **Mix Shader** node is used to mix two shaders. You can connect the first shader to the top slot and the second shader to the bottom slot.

Fac controls how you want the mixture to go. The 0.5 default value means that the mixture will be even, meaning that the output shader will have 50% of the first shader and 50% of the second shader. If you set it to 0.25, it means that the output shader will have 75% of the first shader and only 25% of the second, and so on.

Let's connect **Glass BSDF** to the top of **Mix Shader** and **Transparent BSDF** to the bottom. Then, we will connect the right-hand slot of **Mix Shader** to **Material Output**.

9. Connect the **Glass BSDF** right slot to the **Surface** slot on **Material Output**.

10. For the **Fac** amount, we'll go with 0.25, meaning that we'll be using 25% of **Transparent BSDF** and 75% of **Glass BSDF**.

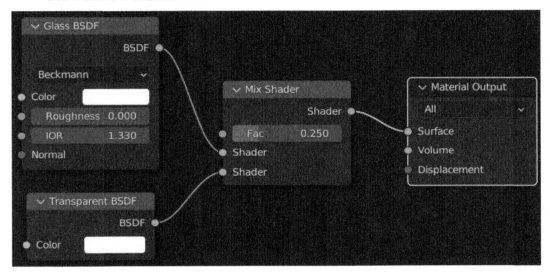

Figure 7.8 – Mixing Glass BSDF and Transparent BSDF using Mix Shader

Next, we need to tweak the color of our water material. To do, that let's perform these actions:

1. Add a **ColorRamp** node.

2. Connect the right-hand **Color** slot of **ColorRamp** to both **Glass BSDF** and **Transparent BSDF**.

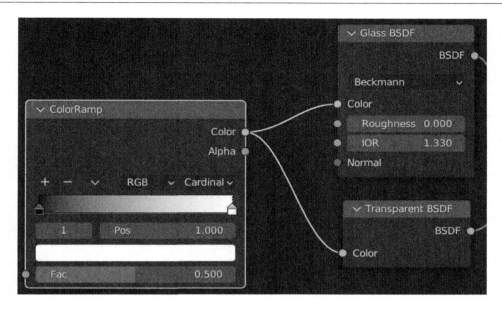

Figure 7.9 – Adding a ColorRamp node and connecting it to Glass BSDF and Transparent BSDF

3. In **ColorRamp**, we need to have four handles to work with, so let's add an additional two handles by clicking on the plus symbol.

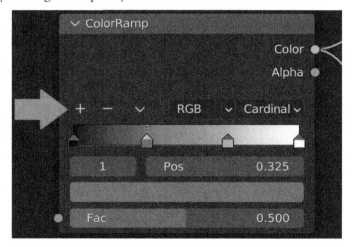

Figure 7.10 – Adding two additional handles to the ColorRamp node

4. Make sure that the distance between the four handles is the same.

The next step is to color our water. To do that, we'll be using the water colors palette shown in the following figure, which gives us a variety of ocean colors based on how deep the water is.

Figure 7.11 – Ocean blue palette used to create river water

This ocean blue color palette is made up of multiple shades of blue, which includes ocean colors, from dark blue, which is how the deepest points of the ocean look, to light gray-blue, which we see on the surface of the ocean.

We need to feed this ocean blue color palette to our **ColorRamp** node to achieve a photorealistic water shader.

So, let's add four blue shades with the color hex codes to our **ColorRamp** node.

Note

Keep in mind that this method is not a real representation of how water works in real life. In fact, the perceived color of water is a complex mix of both refracted and reflected light from the environment. Here, we're just trying to create a nice water shade that looks as realistic as possible in our landscape environment.

---

5.   Select the first handle and click on the bottom color.

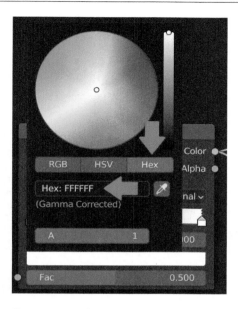

Figure 7.12 – Changing the Hex color code

6. Switch to **Hex** and enter the following hex codes for each of the four handles' colors:

    • **Color 1**: Dark blue – **#112945**

    • **Color 2**: Yale blue – **#4C6381**

    • **Color 3**: Turquoise blue – **#5E6F82**

    • **Color 4**: Light blue – **#D6DEFF**

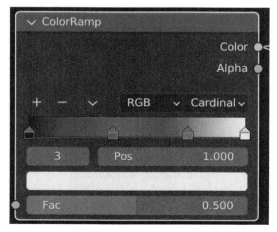

Figure 7.13 – Adding four colors to ColorRamp

7. Now, if we jump into the **Rendered** view by pressing *Z* on the 3D Viewport, we'll see those colors applied to the surface of our water.

Figure 7.14 – A rendered preview of the landscape scene with a river

However, the surface of the water looks 100% flat and smooth, so we need to add small waves to make it look like real river water.

Adding waves to the water's surface

To add waves to our water, we need to use the **Noise Texture** node:

1. Press *Shift + A* in **Shader Editor** and search for Noise Texture.

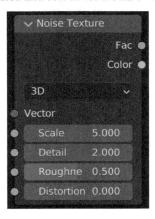

Figure 7.15 –Noise Texture

2. To connect **Noise Texture** to a **Displacement** node, let's search for the `Displacement` node.

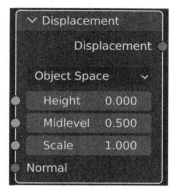

Figure 7.16 – Displacement node

3. Connect the **Fac** slot of **Noise Texture** to the **Height** slot for **Displacement**.

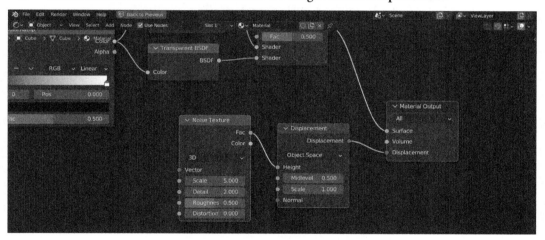

Figure 7.17 – Connecting Noise Texture to the Displacement slot

This is the effect the **Noise Texture** node is applying to our water; it's strangely warping the surface.

Figure 7.18 – A rendered preview of the landscape scene with a river

The reason it looks like this is because of the low scale under **Scale** on **Noise Texture**, so we need to increase **Scale** to around 200.000. It might be a different value based on your own setup, so just adjust coordinately until you have a nice-looking wave effect.

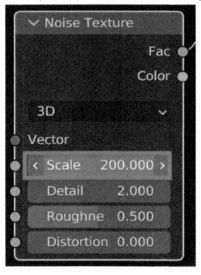

Figure 7.19 – Increasing Scale for Noise Texture

However, the problem is that this noise effect on the surface of the water is too strong; we need to reduce its strength. You can see in the figure here that the water waves don't give us a good reflection of the landscape on the water.

Figure 7.20 – A rendered preview of the landscape scene with a river

In order to fix this problem, let's reduce the **Scale** value of the **Displacement** node to 0.400.

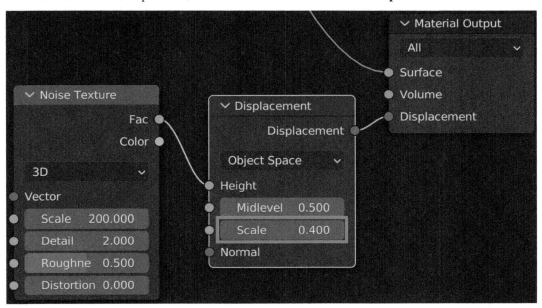

Figure 7.21 – Dropping the Displacement node between Noise Texture and Material Output

4. Let's jump into the **Rendered** view by pressing Z on the 3D Viewport; we'll see those nice waves applied to the surface of our water.

Figure 7.22 – A rendered preview of the landscape scene with a river

Now, this is how our **Water** material looks; it has a subtle wave effect on the surface of it that looks great. However, if we pay attention to the water surface when animating it, the wave effect will be fixed, which looks unnatural, so we need to animate the waves.

Animating the water flow

We will have a look at a cool trick that will allow us to animate our water surface, making the waves move:

1. Add **Mapping** and **Texture Coordinate** nodes.
2. Connect the **Generated** slot on the **Texture Coordinate** node to **Vector** on the left side of the **Mapping** node.
3. Connect the right-hand **Vector** slot of the **Mapping** node to **Vector** on **Noise Texture**.

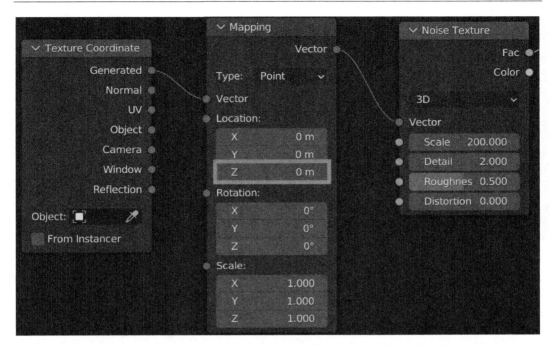

Figure 7.23 – Adding the Mapping and Texture Coordinate nodes to Noise Texture

Now, if you change the value of the **Z** location on the **Mapping** node, you will notice that **Noise Texture** is moving.

4. To animate the **Z** location value on **Mapping**, we need access to the **Timeline** editor, so hover your mouse over the bottom-right window, left-click, and drag upward.

    This will give you a new duplicated window of **Shader Editor**. Let's switch it to the **Timeline** editor and jump into the first frame:

    Timeline is identified by a clock icon; it is used for manipulating keyframes. **Keyframes** give specific information about a certain object at a certain time. Think of this like a person holding a GPS device and going from place to place, from a coffee shop to a restaurant and then to the car parking lot. At each time, we can locate their position and write down the time that the person was there.

    In the **Timeline** editor, you can see the keyframes as diamond shapes. We're not seeing them because we haven't inserted any details about any object.

    Let's switch from the **Shader Editor** window to **Timeline,** as shown in the figure here:

Figure 7.24 – Switching to Timeline

5.   Now, go to the **Shader Editor** window, find the **Mapping** node, and right-click on the **Z** location value:

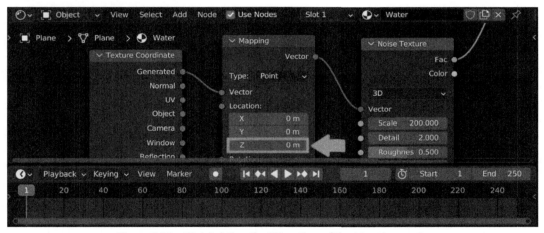

Figure 7.25 – Highlighting the Z location of the Mapping node

By right-clicking on the **Z** location value, you will get access to this menu:

Figure 7.26 – Inserting the keyframes of the Mapping node's Z location

6. Click on **Insert Keyframes** and you will have a new keyframe inserted into the first frame of the **Timeline** editor. This means that, in the first frame of our animation, the **Z** location of the **Mapping** node is set to 0 m.

Immediately, a keyframe will show in the **Timeline** editor in the form of a yellow diamond shape.

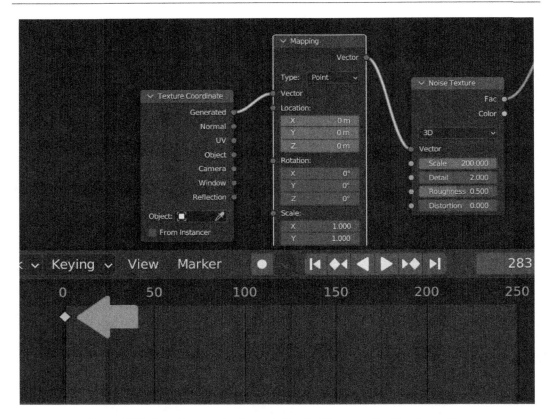

Figure 7.27 – Inserting one keyframe in the first frame on the Timeline editor

If you're not seeing it, this means that the **Mapping** node isn't selected. Make sure to left-click on the **Mapping** node in **Shader Editor** to be able to see the keyframe diamond shape in the **Timeline** editor.

7. Now, let's jump to frame 100.

Figure 7.28 – Jumping to frame 100 on the Timeline editor

8. Let's increase the **Z** location of **Mapping** to 1 m by right-clicking on the **Z** location and selecting **Insert Keyframes**.

Now, we have inserted two keyframes:

- The first keyframe is on frame **1**; it has the **Z** value of the **Mapping** node set to 0 m

- The second keyframe is on frame **100**; it has the **Z** value of the **Mapping** node set to 1 m

Once you have inserted both keyframes, the **Timeline** editor will have two diamond shapes for keyframes **1** and **100** like so:

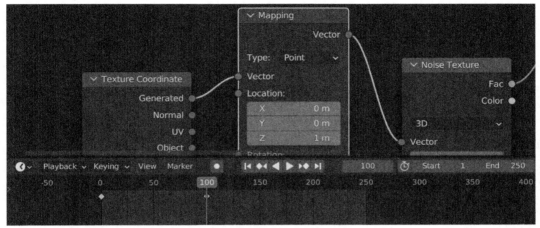

Figure 7.29 – Inserting the second keyframe into the 100th frame on the Timeline editor

In general, the keyframes contribute to actual time. In the **Output Properties** tab, we have a setting called **Frame Rate** – this controls how timeline frame numbers relate to actual time.

By default, we have **Frame Rate** set to **24 fps**, meaning that we have 24 frames per second.

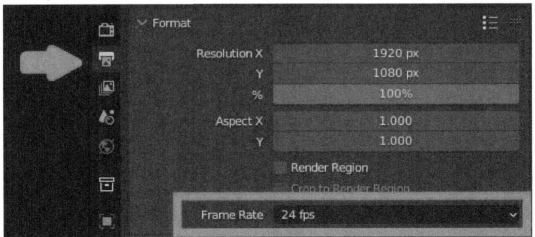

Figure 7.30 – Checking Frame Rate under Output Properties

So, in our example, we're moving the water surface waves by 1 meter at a time interval of 4 seconds (100 frames divided by 24 fps).

The water animation will stop at frame **100**, but how can we make it cyclic and continuous? Let's figure that out.

Creating a continuously looping animation

The last thing to do is to make our wave movement continuous. So far, it stops at frame **100**, which means that at frame **100**, or 4 seconds after playing the animation, the water will freeze again.

To make this animation cyclic, press *Shift + E* on the **Timeline** editor and select **Make Cyclic (F-Modifier)**.

Figure 7.31 – Making the animation cyclic by pressing Shift + E on the Timeline editor

Basically, that's it. Our animation now is cyclic. We can press the play icon at the top right of the **Timeline** editor to play the animation.

Summary

In this chapter, we went through the process of creating a realistic water shader and applying it to our river. We learned how to mix between the **Glass BSDF** and **Transparency BSDF** nodes to create a nice reflective and refractive surface. Then, we added a subtle wave effect on the surface of the water using **Noise Texture**. Finally, we learned how to animate the waves on the surface by inserting keyframes into the **Timeline** editor.

In the next chapter, we'll improve the texture of our landscape by using two textures: mud and grass. We will learn how to use **Texture Paint** to brush nice-looking mud and grass onto our landscape.

8

Creating Procedural Mud Material

In this chapter, we will be creating a realistic mud material using procedural texturing and using it to texture the bottom of the landscape that we created in the previous chapter. You will learn how to create and combine many different layers of details, such as adding water puddles, stones, and mud details, and combining all these details into one complex, realistic result.

We will tap into the unlimited potential of Blender's incredibly powerful node editor and learn how to create advanced and highly customizable procedural textures from scratch.

We will learn how to keep our node setup organized and easy to use.

In this chapter, we'll be covering the following topic:

- Creating a realistic mud material using procedural texturing in Blender

Technical requirements

This chapter requires a Mac or PC capable of running Blender Version 3.0 or above.

You can download the resources for this chapter from GitHub at `https://github.com/PacktPublishing/3D-Environment-Design-with-Blender/tree/main/chapter-8`

Creating a realistic mud material using procedural texturing in Blender

Let's create the mud material using procedural texturing in Blender – but first, we need to understand the nature of mud. If we break down mud, we will find that it is a combination of soil, stones, loam, and other stuff, and everything is mixed with water, so these are the elements that we will be creating procedurally in Blender:

- Water puddles
- Soil
- Stones

To keep you motivated, this is the final result that you'll be able to achieve by the end of this chapter:

Figure 8.1 – The final result of the mud material that you will achieve

You can skip this chapter and use the final result by downloading the Blender file that you will find at this GitHub link: https://github.com/PacktPublishing/3D-Environment-Design-with-Blender/blob/c9a6c37ca19a618bec29ac0e0f9a39576c9883ad/chapter-8/Procedural%20Mud%20Material.zip.

Let's get started with the creation of our mud material.

Creating the mud material

To create the mud material, let's launch a new Blender scene and add a sphere object by pressing *Shift + A* and choosing **Sphere**. The **Sphere** object has nothing to do with our landscape project – it's just a way to display the mud material. We will get rid of it later once we assign the mud to the landscape.

By default, the **Sphere** object will have wireframes visible on it, so we need to smooth it out. To smooth the mesh and hide the edge lines, right-click on the sphere and choose **Shade Smooth**, as you can see in the following figure.

With the **Sphere** object selected, go to **Material Properties** and add a new material called Mud:

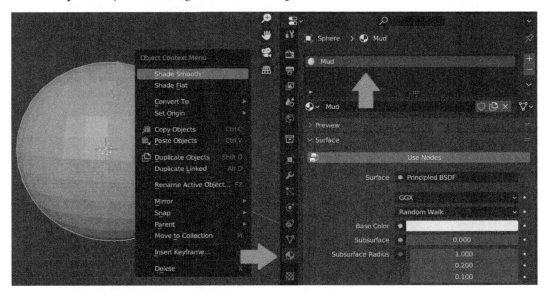

Figure 8.2 – Using Shade Smooth on the Sphere object and adding a material called Mud

Switch the bottom window from the default Timeline to **Shader Editor** so that we can start working on the **Mud** material. By default, you will have the **Principled BSDF** node connected to **Material Output**:

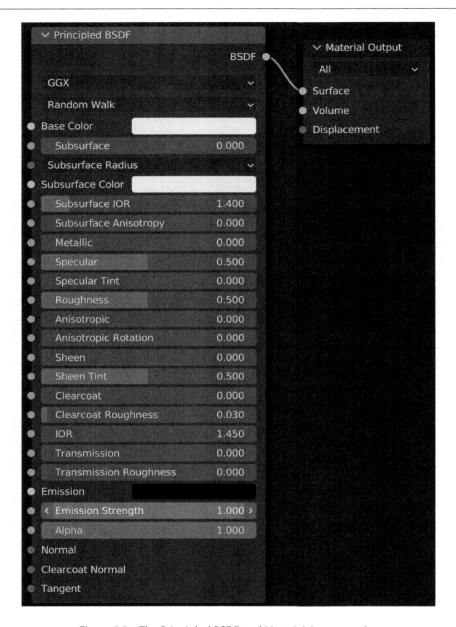

Figure 8.3 – The Principled BSDF and Material Output nodes

Now that we have created our material and assigned it to the **Sphere** object, let's start with the first step of creating the **Mud** material, which is adding water puddles.

Creating water puddles for the mud material

To create water puddles, perform the following steps:

1. Add **Noise Texture** in **Shader Editor** and increase the **Detail** value to 7.5.

2. Add a **ColorRamp** node and connect **Noise Texture** to it.

3. For the position of the handles, select the white handle and set the **Pos** value to 0.45, and set the black handle to 0.6:

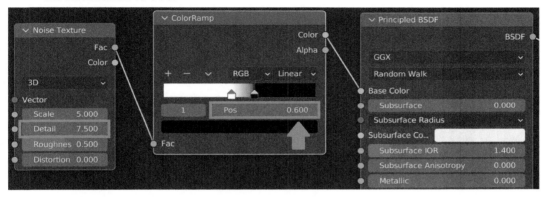

Figure 8.4 – Connecting Noise Texture to ColorRamp and then to Principled BSDF

4. Change the color of black handle to light gray by setting the **V** value to 0.180:

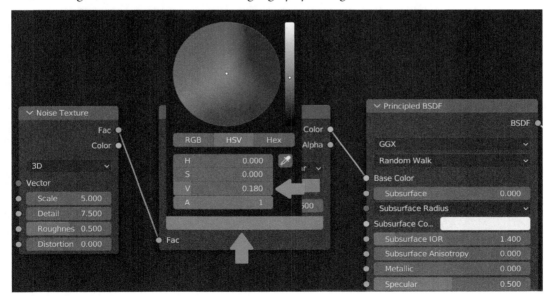

Figure 8.5 – Changing the color of the ColorRamp handles

Now, to check the material, let's go back to the 3D Viewport, press *Z*, and switch to **Material Preview** so that we can see our progress with the mud material. This is how our material looks:

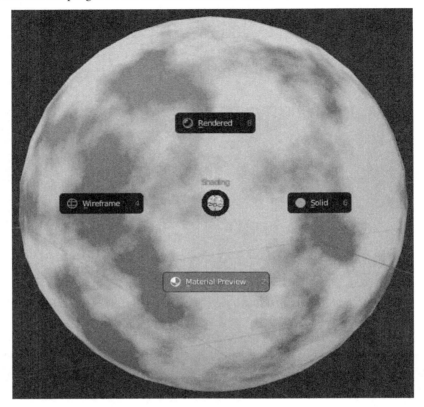

Figure 8.6 – Water Puddles node setup applied to the sphere

It looks like a moon – don't worry about that. All we need for now are those white and gray spots. Later, we'll be using these spots to separate the mud from the water, and it will look awesome – promise.

For now, before we proceed with more details and make our node setup large and confusing, we need to find a way to organize it, so let's learn about the **Frame** node.

Organizing the node setup using the Frame node

Frame is a node used for organizing nodes by collecting related nodes together in a common area. You can give this area a specific name and a particular color to make it different from the other frames.

To keep our node setup organized, we'll put the **Water Puddles** nodes that we created inside a **Frame** node, so in **Shader Editor**, press *Shift + A*, go to **Layout**, and click on **Frame**. You will get a small empty black frame.

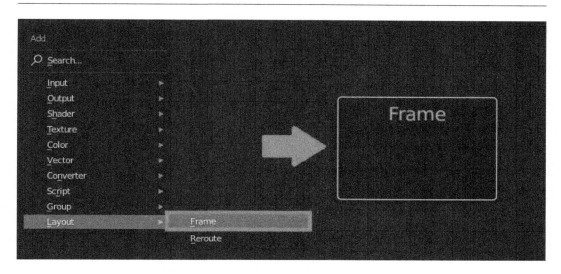

Figure 8.7 – Adding a Frame node to organize the node setup

Now, let's select the **Noise Texture** and **ColorRamp** nodes and drag them inside the frame by pressing *G*.

We can also change the label name on the top of our frame by pressing *N* to access the left panel and changing the **Label** text to Water Puddles, or anything you want.

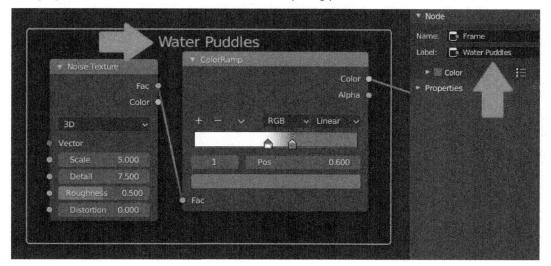

Figure 8.8 – Putting Noise Texture and ColorRamp inside a frame and calling it Water Puddles

Now that we have organized the water puddles nodes inside a **Frame** node, let's add small stone details to our mud material.

Adding stones to the Mud material

To add stones, we'll be using a different texture node called **Musgrave**.

Musgrave Texture is a node used to add an advanced procedural noise texture. It's a type of **Fractal Noise** that generates noise with different scaling. We'll be using it to generate stones with different scales.

To add **Musgrave Texture**, press *Shift + A* and search for Musgrave Texture. Connect it to a **ColorRamp** node, as we did with **Noise Texture**.

For the **Musgrave Texture** settings, follow these steps:

1. Set the **Scale** value to 25.
2. Increase **Detail** to 5.
3. For the **Dimension** setting, increase it to 1.5.

Next, we will connect **Musgrave Texture** to a **ColorRamp** node. For the **ColorRamp** settings, follow these steps:

1. Change the gray handle position to 0.45.
2. For the color of the black handle, change the **V** value to 0.13. Check *Figure 8.5* to see where to find the **V** value:

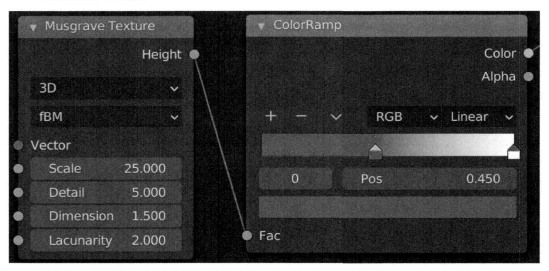

Figure 8.9 – Adding Musgrave Texture and connecting it to ColorRamp

3. Now to see the stones, let's disconnect the **Water Puddles** node setup and connect **ColorRamp** to **BaseColor** on the **Principled BSDF** node instead. This connection is temporary – the purpose of it is to see separately how **Musgrave Texture** behaves with the **ColorRamp** node.

This is how **Musgrave Texture** behaves with **ColorRamp**:

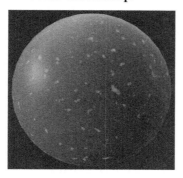

Figure 8.10 – Displaying large stone details

We'll be adding two types of stones to our **Mud** material – small stones and big ones. Variation is key to achieving a photorealistic material, so let's select **Musgrave Texture**, along with **ColorRamp**, and press *Shift + D* to duplicate them twice. You can press *G* to move the new duplicated nodes down.

This time, we'll increase the **Scale** setting of **Musgrave Texture** to 75 – the goal is to have small stones.

Next, we need to combine both **Musgrave Texture** nodes by using a **MixRGB** node. In **Shader Editor**, search for a `MixRGB` node and connect the first **ColorRamp** node to the first slot of **MixRGB**, and then do the same thing for the second **ColorRamp** node. You can see the node setup in the following figure:

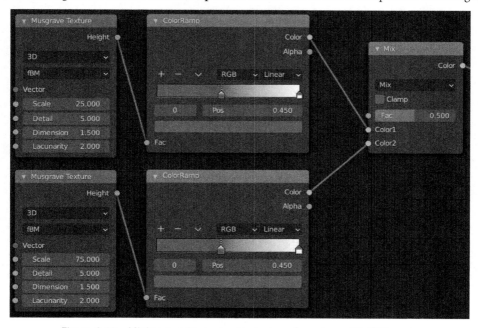

Figure 8.11 – Mixing two Musgrave Texture nodes using a MixRGB node

Let's take a look at our material right now in the 3D Viewport:

Figure 8.12 – Mixing small stones with large ones

As you can see, there's a combination of small and large spots. They will serve later as small stones.

Let's add a frame, call it `Stones` to keep everything organized, and put both **Musgrave Texture** nodes with **ColorRamp** into it.

There is also the possibility to change the color of the frame to make it different from other frames. Just press *N* to access the right-hand panel and check the **Color** checkbox below **Label**. Then, you can choose any color you want. In my case, I went with red to color the **Stones** frame. You can see this in the following figure:

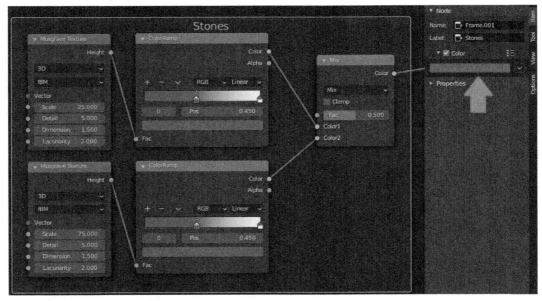

Figure 8.13 – Changing the color of the Stones node frame

Now, let's combine the **Stones** node setup with the puddles.

Combining the stones with the puddles

To combine the **Stones** node setup with the puddles, let's use the **MixRGB** node:

1. Add the **MixRGB** node.

2. Set the mixing type to **Multiply**.

3. Set the mixing amount to 0.85 so that we can have 85% puddles and 25% stones.

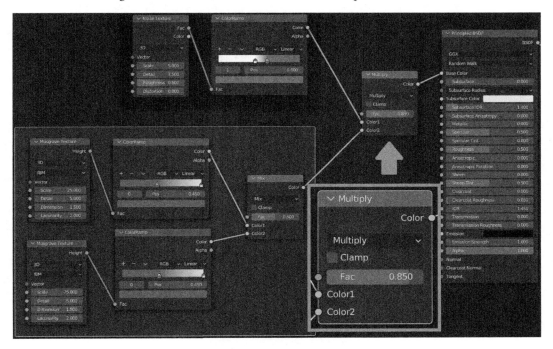

Figure 8.14 – Combining water puddles with stones using the MixRGB node

After combining the stones with the puddles, let's add more details to our mud material.

Adding mud details

If we check our current material, we will find some smooth spots that have no details.

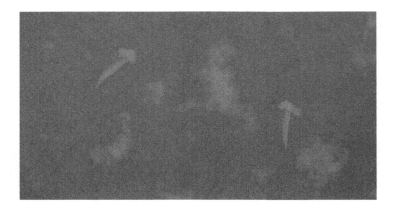

Figure 8.15 – Highlighting empty areas in our Mud material

We need to fill these areas. To do that, we'll be using a **Noise Texture** node, so press *Shift + A* and add **Noise Texture**.

Set the **Noise Texture** node to the following:

1. Change **Scale** to 1.

2. Increase the **Detail** value to 7.5.

3. Increase **Roughness** to 1.

Figure 8.16 – The Noise Texture node

Now, we need to mix the **Water Puddles** and **Stones** node setup with this new **Noise Texture**. Add a new **MixRGB** node and set it to the following:

1. Keep the mixing type as **Multiply**.

2. Set the mixing value to 0.9:

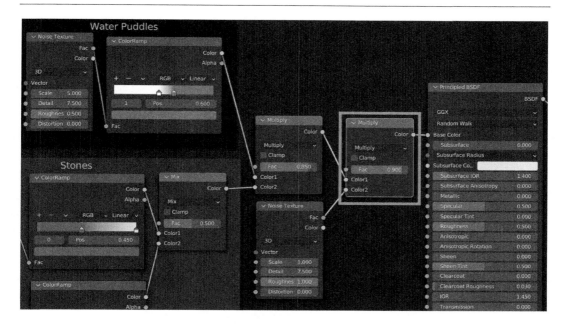

Figure 8.17 – Mud material node setup

And this is how our material looks so far:

Figure 8.18 – Mud material with water puddles and stones applied

This node setup is the mud core – next, we'll be using this core to generate the mud color, reflection or roughness, and bump details. Let's start by adding the mud color.

Adding color to the mud material

Mud is always a kind of brown. To achieve a brownish color, let's add a **ColorRamp** node and set it to the following settings:

1. Click on the plus sign so that we can have three handles:

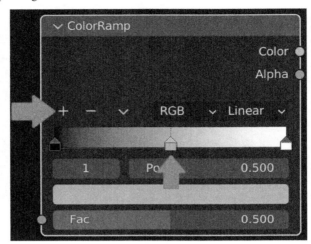

Figure 8.19 – Adding a third handle to ColorRamp

2. Select the first handle on the right-hand side. Click on the handle color below and change the following values:

   - The **H** value to 0.14
   - The **S** value to 0.22
   - The **V** value to 0.08

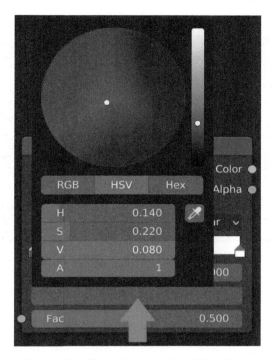

Figure 8.20 – Changing the color of ColorRamp

3. Next, select the middle handle on the right-hand side, change the **Pos** value to 0.17, and set the handle color to the following values:

    - The **H** value to 0.03
    - The **S** value to 0.6
    - The **V** value to 0.03

4. For the third handle, set the **Pos** value to 0.227, and the handle color details to the following:

    - The **H** value to 0.08
    - The **S** value to 0.288
    - The **V** value to 0.1

    This is how **ColorRamp** should look:

Figure 8.21 – The ColorRamp node

Now, let's connect the last **MixRGB** node, the one with the **Multiply** mixing type and the 0.9 **Fac** value, to the left-hand side of the preceding **ColorRamp** node, and connect the right-hand side of the **ColorRamp** node to the **Principled BDSF**'s **BaseColor** slot as follows:

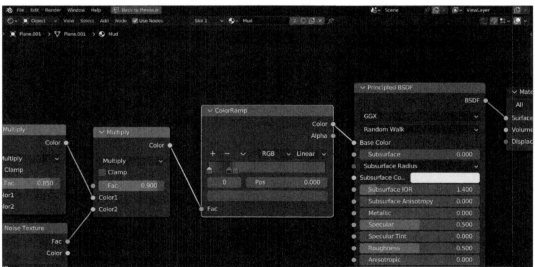

Figure 8.22 – Connecting ColorRamp to Base Color

In case you want to see the entire node setup, this is how it looks:

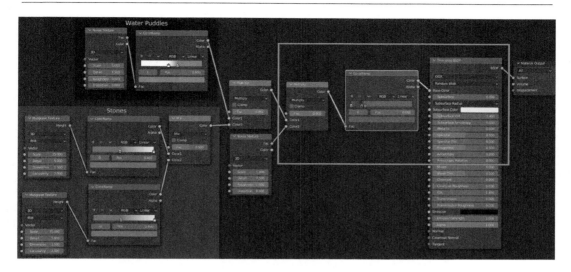

Figure 8.23 – Full node setup of the Mud node, highlighting the ColorRamp node connected to Base Color

And this is how our material will look when we connect **ColorRamp** to the **Base Color** slot of **Principled BSDF**:

Figure 8.24 – Mud material with the Base Color map applied

Now we have the mud material color, the next step is to work on the material reflection, which involves the **Roughness** map.

Adding reflection to the mud material

We need to make the water puddles reflective to light, while the mud spots need to be less reflective. To achieve this goal, let's add another **ColorRamp** node and set it to the following:

- Select the first black handle and set the **Pos** value to 0.05.

- For the second white handle, change its **Pos** value to 0.2, click on its color, and change the **V** value to 0.62 to make the white color look gray. This is how the **ColorRamp** node should look:

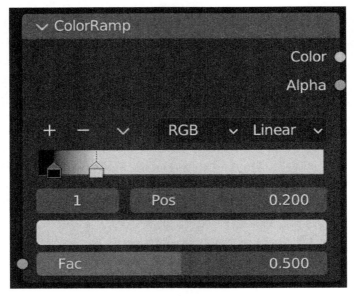

Figure 8.25 – The ColorRamp node

Now, let's connect the last **MixRGB** node, the one with the **Multiply** mixing type and the0.9 **Fac** value, to the left-hand side of this **ColorRamp** node, and connect the right-hand side of the **ColorRamp** node to **Principled BDSF's Roughness** slot as follows:

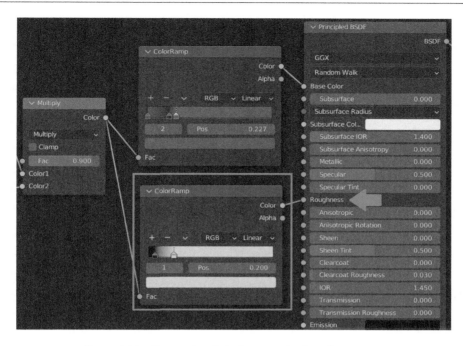

Figure 8.26 – Connecting ColorRamp to the Roughness map

In case you want to see the entire node setup, this is how it looks:

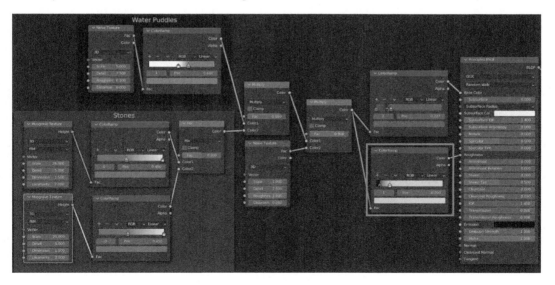

Figure 8.27 – Full node setup of the Mud node, highlighting the
ColorRamp node connected to the Roughness map

This is how our material will look with **Roughness** applied:

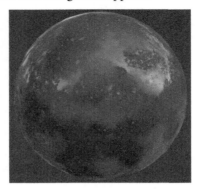

Figure 8.28 - Mud material with the Roughness map applied

We have the mud color with the right reflection that separates the water puddles from the mud. Our next move is to add bump details.

Adding bumps to the mud material

To add mud bumps, we'll be using a new **ColorRamp** node. Add it and set it to the following settings:

1. Select the first black handle and set its **Pos** value to 0.1.

2. For the second handle, change the **Pos** value to 0.47 and its **V** color value to 0.62.

   It should look like this:

Figure 8.29 – The ColorRamp node

Now let's put this **ColorRamp** nodeto work.

In order to connect this **ColorRamp** node to the **Normal** channel on **Principled BSDF**, we need to convert it into a **Normal** map first. To do that, we'll be using a new node called **Bump**. Let's search for this Bump node; this is how it looks:

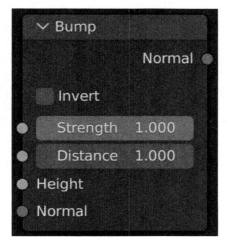

Figure 8.30 – The Bump node

Now, let's connect the last **MixRGB** node, the one with the **Multiply** mixing type and the 0.9 **Fac** value, to the left-hand side of this **ColorRamp** node, and connect the right-hand side of the **ColorRamp** node to the **Bump** node's **Height** slot as follows:

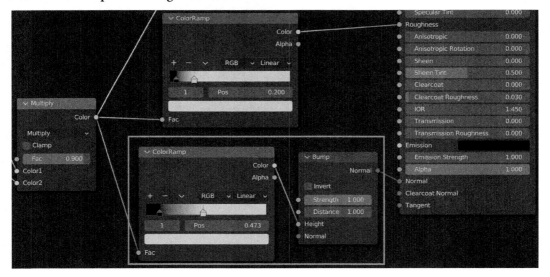

Figure 8.31 – Connecting the ColorRamp node to the Bump node

This is the full node setup:

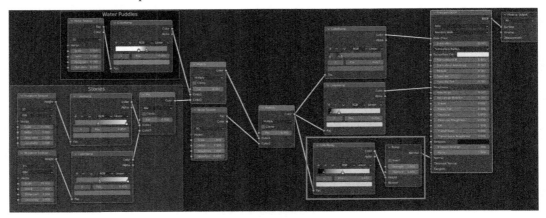

Figure 8.32 – Full node setup of the Mud node, highlighting the
ColorRamp node connected to the Bump node

Make sure to also reduce the **Strength** value of the **Bump** node to 0.25 to generate subtle bumps. Now, if we go back to the 3D Viewport, this is how our material looks:

Figure 8.33 – Mud material with the Bumps map applied

Alright – we applied the bumps to our mud material, so the next step is to add real geometry details by using the **Displacement** map.

Adding displacement to the mud material

Before we can dive into the creation of the **Displacement** map, let's understand **displacement mapping** first.

Displacement mapping allows a texture to manipulate the position of vertices on rendered geometry. Unlike **Normal** or **Bump** mapping, where the shading is distorted to give the illusion of bumps, **Displacement** maps create real bumps.

To add displacement details, first, we need to switch the render engine to **Cycles**. You can do that by accessing **Render Properties** in the right-hand panel as shown here:

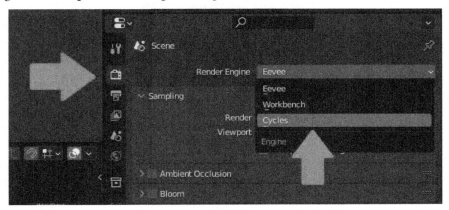

Figure 8.34 – Switching the render engine to Cycles

Next, with the sphere selected, go to **Material Properties**, and scroll down to **Settings**. On the **Surface** tab, you'll find **Displacement** – click on it and change it to **Displacement and Bump** as follows:

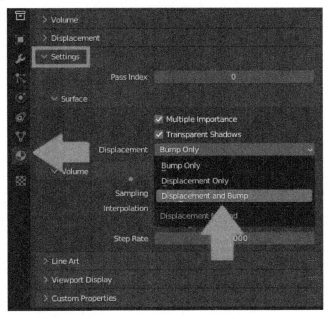

Figure 8.35 – Switching the Displacement type from Bump Only to Displacement and Bump

Now, let's go back to the **Mud** node setup, and let's add a new node called **Displacement**:

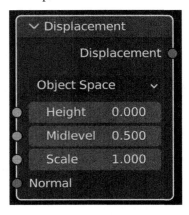

Figure 8.36 – The Displacement node

To control this **Displacement** node, let's add a **ColorRamp** node and set it to the following settings:

1. Select the black handle and make it completely white by setting its **V** value to 1.

2. Select the second handle and set its **Pos** value to 0.56 and its **V** value to 0.81.

This is how the **ColorRamp** node should look:

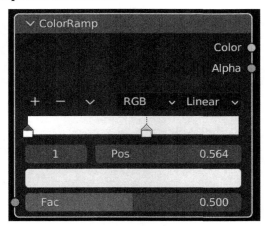

Figure 8.37 – The ColorRamp node

This **ColorRamp** node will do two things to our mud material:

-   First, it will reduce the strength of the displacement

-   Second, it will remove the displacement details from the **Water Puddles** areas to keep them flat

The sphere on the left-hand side of the figure here has no **ColorRamp** node applied while the one on the right has **ColorRamp** applied:

Figure 8.38 – The difference between not using and using the ColorRamp node on the mud material

Now we need to use the first **Noise Texture** node we used to create the water puddles as a map for the displacement, so let's connect **Noise Texture** straight to **ColorRamp**.

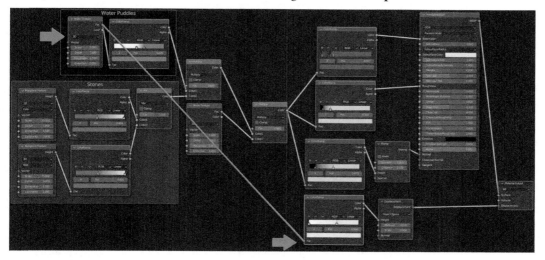

Figure 8.39 – Full node setup of the mud material

Now, the **Displacement** map of our **mud** material is working. In order to see it working, we need to switch to the **Render** mode, but before doing that, let's improve the lighting of our scene.

Setting good lighting in our scene

To change the lighting of our scene, we need to switch **Shader Editor** to **World**. At the top of **Shader Editor**, we have the option to switch from the **Object** mode to the **World** mode, and the **World** mode is where we can adjust the lighting of our environment.

That being said, let's switch to **World** as shown in the figure here:

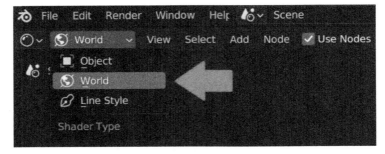

Figure 8.40 – Switching the Shader Editor mode from Object to World

By default, you will find two nodes: **Background** and **World Output**. Let's search for and add a new node called Sky Texture and connect it to the **Background** node, as shown in *Figure 8.41*.

Make sure to also reduce the **Strength** value of the **Background** node to 0.5 and connect the nodes as follows:

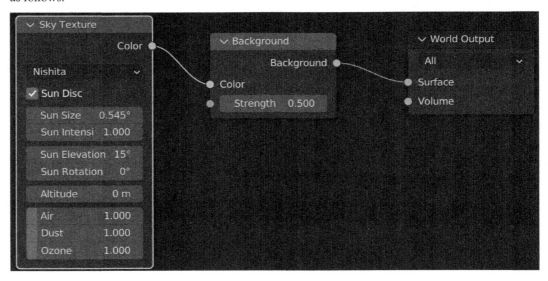

Figure 8.41 – Setting the Sky Texture lighting

Now, let's go back to the 3D Viewport and switch the shading mode to **Rendered** by pressing *Z* and choosing **Rendered**. This is what the mud material will look like:

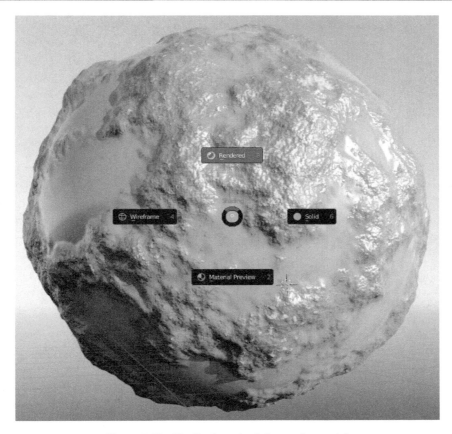

Figure 8.42 – The final result of the mud material

Basically, there we go! We created a nice-looking, realistic mud material using procedural texturing in Blender. It's time to use the mud material we created to texture the bottom section of the landscape.

For now, you can save this Blender file as `Procedural Mud Material` – we will be using this Blender file in the next chapter.

Summary

In this chapter, we went through the process of creating a realistic mud material using procedural texturing in Blender. We learned how to create water puddles by combining **Noise Texture** with a **ColorRamp** node, adding stone details by using **Musgrave Texture**, organizing our node setup by adding **Frame** nodes, adding color to the mud material, adding reflection, bumps, and a **Displacement** map, and finally, we applied nice lighting to render the mud on the sphere.

In the next chapter, we'll be creating an organic mask and using the mud material we created to texture the bottom section of our landscape.

9

Texturing the Landscape with Mud Material

In this chapter, we will be texturing the landscape by mixing two different materials, the rocky snow and the mud we created in the previous chapter. To do that, we will be using a mask that separates the rocky snow from the mud in an organic, nice-looking way.

You will be comfortable with mixing two different materials on the same object while controlling where and to what degree you want the mixing to occur. Being able to mix different materials is a great skill that helps you generate unique materials and apply them to your objects.

In the second part of this chapter, you will learn how to optimize and organize your node setup by using groups. This is an important skill to acquire when working with complex material nodes. Node grouping will allow you to simplify a node tree by hiding away complexity.

You will learn to pack all your nodes related to a specific material into a single group node that only has the essential parameters you need.

In this chapter, we'll be covering the following topics:

- Importing the **Mud** material
- Creating a **Texturing** mask

Technical requirements

This chapter requires a Mac or PC capable of running Blender Version 3.0 or above.

Importing the Mud material

The first thing we need to do is to import the **Mud** material into the landscape scene, so let's go back to the landscape scene from *Chapter 7. Creating and Animating Realistic, Natural-Looking Water*. In this scene, we don't have the **Mud** material – we have only the rocky snow material applied to the landscape.

This is how the landscape looks so far with the rocky snow material applied:

Figure 9.1 – Final result of the landscape from Chapter 7

To import the **Mud** material, we'll be using the **Append** feature.

The **Append** feature allows us to reuse materials, objects, and other data loaded from another Blender file.

Let's use the **Append** feature to import the mud material:

1.   At the top of the Blender scene, go to **File** and choose **Append**.

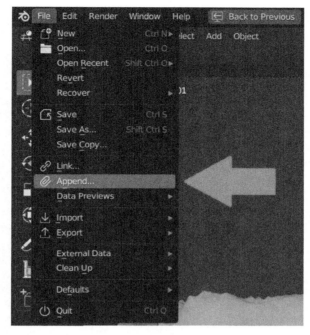

Figure 9.2 – Clicking on the Append feature

2. A small window will pop up, allowing you to browse your files – choose the mud material Blender file and click on it.

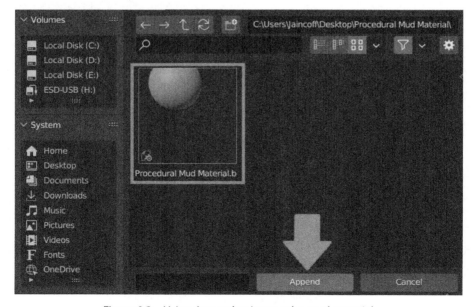

Figure 9.3 – Using Append to import the mud material

3.   You will have access to multiple folders, and since what we need to import is a material, we need to choose the **Material** folder.

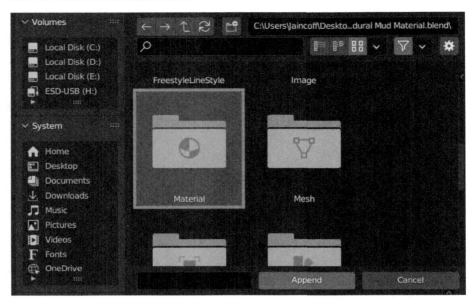

Figure 9.4 – Clicking on the Material folder to import the mud material

Then, you will find the material we're looking for, **Mud** – click on it and choose **Append**.

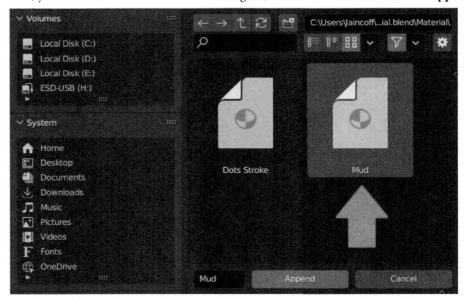

Figure 9.5 – Using Append to import the Mud material

And now the **Mud** material is part of our **Material** library. Let's add **Mud** to the landscape materials collection:

1. Select the landscape object.
2. Go to **Material Properties**.
3. Add new material and choose **Mud**.

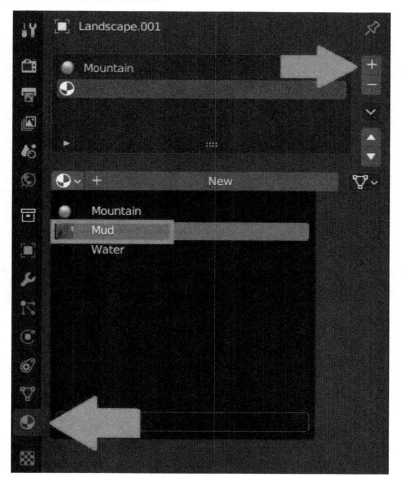

Figure 9.6 – Adding the Mud material to the landscape

Now, we have the **Mud** material as part of the landscape materials – you won't see any change to the landscape yet because we didn't assign the **Mud** material, but before assigning the **Mud** material to the landscape, we need to optimize and organize our **Mud** material in order to manage the nodes well and keep track of them.

Using groups to organize the Mud node setup

Grouping nodes can simplify a node tree by hiding away complexity. Sometimes, when working on a material, the node tree gets bigger and bigger, which makes controlling the node a difficult task.

This is where node grouping comes in handy. It allows us to combine all the nodes related to a material into a single node that only has the essential parameters we need to customize our material.

To put this in perspective, this is our **Mud** material node setup:

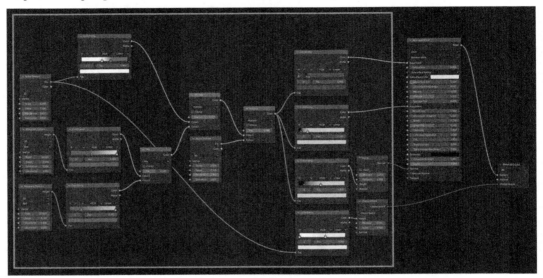

Figure 9.7 – The Mud material node setup

The mud node setup has 16 nodes, and it seems intimidatingly difficult to keep track of every setting. This is how it becomes after grouping all the mud nodes – one single node that only has the parameters we need, **Water Puddles**, **Stones**, and **Mud Noise**:

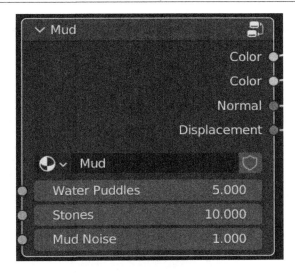

Figure 9.8 – Node group of the Mud material

To group the mud nodes, let's select all the **Mud** material nodes except the **Principled BSDF** and **Material Output** nodes and press *Ctrl + G* just like the green selection in *Figure 9.9*.

When a node group is created, new **Group Input** and **Group Output** nodes will be generated to represent the data flow into and out of the group.

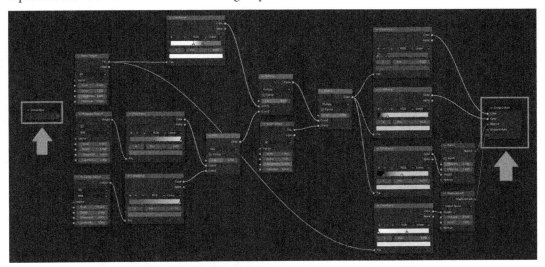

Figure 9.9 – Highlighting Group Input and Group Output

The first node that will appear on the left side of your node setup is **Group Input**. It will be disconnected from the rest.

Group Input is used to store information from the original node setup. You can use it to customize your node setup.

Figure 9.10 – The Group Input node

The second node that you will have when creating a group is **Group Output**. The purpose of the **Group Output** node is to display the result of our node tree. This node has the output slots that we filled in for **Principled BSDF**, which are **Base Color**, **Roughness**, **Normal**, and **Displacement**:

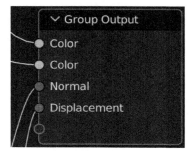

Figure 9.11 – The Group Output node

Now, in order to exit the group node, you can press *Tab* or press the arrow that you will find at the top of your Blender scene:

Figure 9.12 – Arrow symbol to exit the node group

After exiting the group, we will see it as a single node. This way, we transformed the entire **Mud** node setup into a single node that could easily be manipulated.

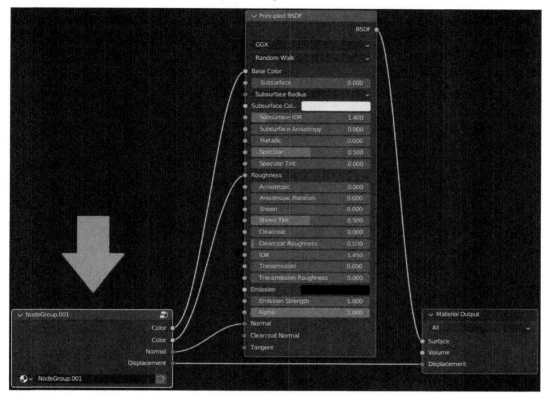

Figure 9.13 – Mud node group

What if we want to change the mud settings? We need to extract the node setup again and tweak the nodes – but what if we could just put the important values that we needed into this node? That is what we will do now.

Adding custom settings to the node group

To add custom settings, we need to go back to the **Group Input** node. First, we need to edit the node group, select the node, right-click on it, and click on **Edit Group**. The hotkey for editing the node group is *Tab*:

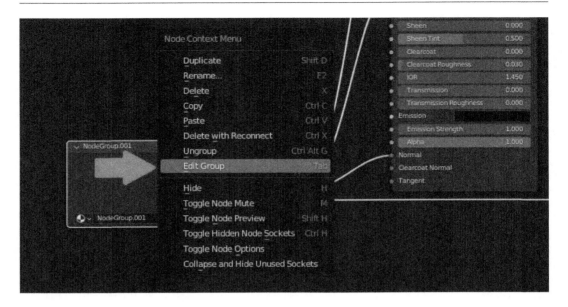

Figure 9.14 – Editing the Mud node group

In our mud example, if we want to pass a parameter related to the **Mud** material into the group, a socket must be added to **Group Input**. To do this, drag a connection from the hollow socket on the right-hand side of the **Group Input** node to the desired input socket of the node requiring an input.

In the example here, we added a parameter to **Group Input** to control the **Scale** value of **Noise Texture**:

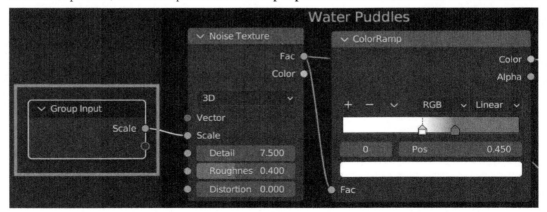

Figure 9.15 – Connecting Group Input to the Noise Texture Scale slot

If we select the **Mud** node group and press *N* to access the right-hand panel, we will have access in **Properties** to **Inputs**.

If you press *N* and go to the **Group** tab, you will be able to change the name of the slot. In our case, I've changed it to `Water Puddles` instead of `Scale`:

- We can change the name of the node group by changing the **Name** value
- We can change the name of the custom setting in the **Group** tab
- **Default** refers to the value you will be seeing by default in the **Mud** node group
- With **Min** and **Max** values, you can set a range that must not be exceeded

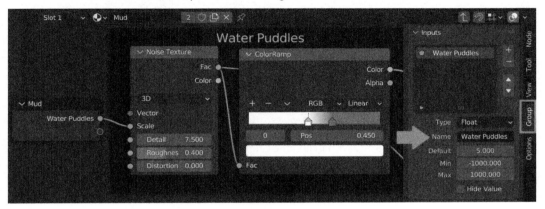

Figure 9.16 – Changing the name of the Mud group node

We also need to change the **Group Output** slot names. In the **Outputs** tab, make sure to change the names of the **Group Output** slots to the following names by order:

- **Base Color**
- **Roughness**
- **Normal**
- **Displacement**

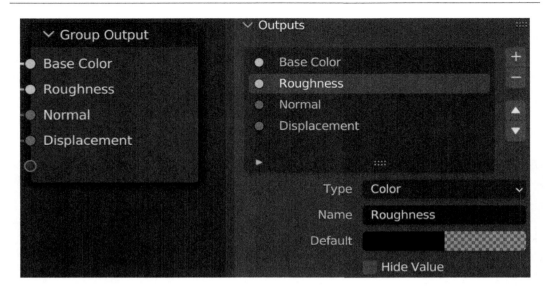

Figure 9.17 – Changing the Group Output slot names

You can add more parameters to the **Mud** group, such as the amount of **Stones** detail and the scale of **Mud Noise** texture. This way, the node group will have the necessary details you need to customize your **Mud** material:

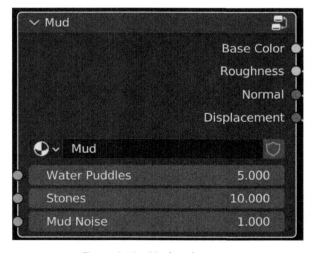

Figure 9.18 – Mud node group

Now that we have imported our **Mud** material and made it a single group node, it will be saved in the node group library. Now, it's time to create the mask that we need to texture our landscape.

Creating a Texturing mask

In nature, snowy mountains melt upside down when they start to melt – meaning that the snow on the mountaintop is the last part of the snow to melt, and as a result of the melting snow, mud is created at the bottom. We will replicate this by creating a mask that allows us to merge the rocky snow and the mud naturally.

A mask is a grayscale texture that determines where and to what degree mixing occurs. Grayscale means black and white.

To create the mask, let's select the landscape object, and then in **Material Properties**, select the **Mountain** material.

Then, make sure to disconnect all the nodes connected to **Principled BSDF** of the **Mountain** material, and please follow these instructions to create the mask:

1. Add a **Texture Coordinate** node.
2. Connect the **Generated** slot of **Texture Coordinate** to a **Separate XYZ** node.
3. Connect **Z** on **Separate XYZ** to a **ColorRamp** node.
4. Add a new handle to **ColorRamp** and color it red.

Separate XYZ separates the landscape mesh based on the colors we have in **ColorRamp**. If you use **Z** on **Separate XYZ**, you will have a vertical distribution of the colors following the *z* axis. The same goes for the other axes – **X** and **Y**.

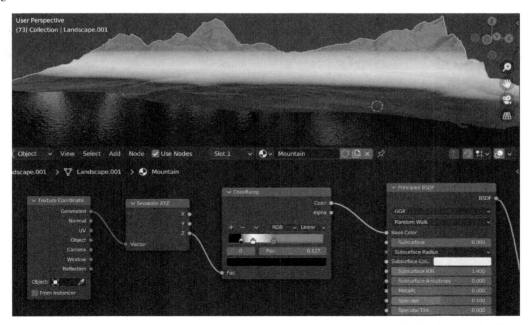

Figure 9.19 – Using the Separate XYZ node to texture the landscape with black, white, and red

In our case, we will need a vertical distribution of materials – snow at the top, and mud at the bottom, so we will keep using the *z* axis for the **Separate XYZ** node.

The red handle was just for demonstrating how the **Separate XYZ** node works. You can delete it by pressing the minus sign on `ColorRamp`. This is what our mask looks like.

We need to move the white and black handles to the left, as shown here:

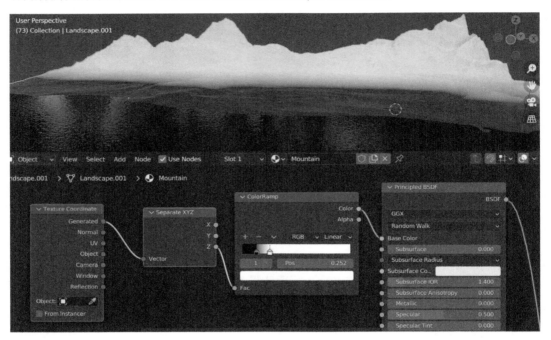

Figure 9.20 – Using the Separate XYZ node to texture the landscape with black and white colors

You can see the edge line – later, we will make the white area snowy and the black area muddy.

For now, we have an issue – the line that separates the black from the white looks smooth. We need to make it look organic and natural. To do that, let's add a **Noise Texture** node and set it to the following settings:

- Set **Scale** to 25.000
- Set **Detail** to 10.000
- Set **Roughness** to 0.700

Then, mix **Noise Texture** with **Separate XYZ** by setting **MixRGB** to **Multiply**:

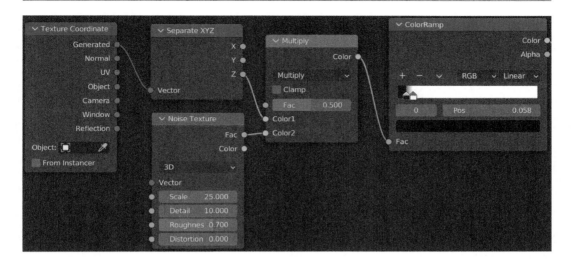

Figure 9.21 – Mixing the Separate XYZ node with Noise Texture

This is how the mountain will look:

Figure 9.22 – Assigning the mask to the landscape

It has a nice organic edge line that will serve as a great separator between the mud and the rocky snow!

To keep our node setup organized, let's put our mask into a group and call the group Mask. Just repeat the same steps we followed before for the **Mud** material.

Figure 9.23 – Node group of the mask

Now, let's go ahead and use this mask to texture our landscape with mud and rocky snow.

Texturing the landscape with mud and rocky snow

Now it's time to use the **Mud** material and the mask we created, but before doing that, let's put the landscape's material called **Mountain** into a group.

Using groups to organize the rocky snow landscape node setup

Let's reconnect the **Mountain** material that we disconnected in the previous *Creating a Texturing mask* section.

Next, let's put the landscape's material called **Mountain** into a group to keep our node setup organized:

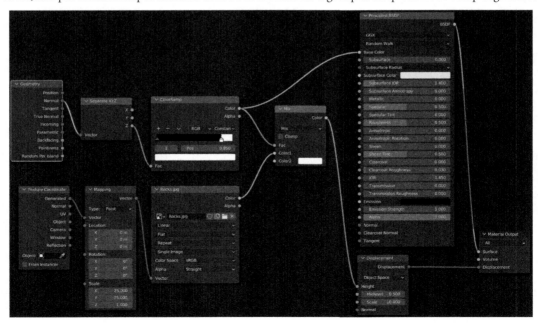

Figure 9.24 – The Mountain node setup

Repeat the same steps we followed for the **Mud** group material – and don't forget to rename the **Group Output** slots of the **Mountain** material please as shown in *Figure 9.17*.

Now we have three node groups: **Mud**, **Mask**, and **Mountain**.

Let's bring in all the node groups we have created – they are saved in Blender nodes now. Press *Shift + A* in **Shader Editor**, go to **Group**, and click on **Mud** and **Mud Mask**:

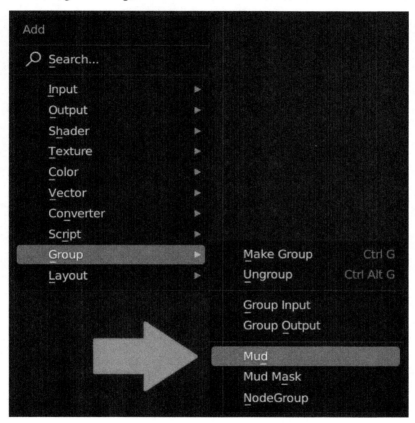

Figure 9.25 – Searching for Mud in Group

Here are all the groups we created. We first have the **Mask** group, the second group is the **Mud** material, and finally, we have the **Mountain** group, which is the snow and rocks combined:

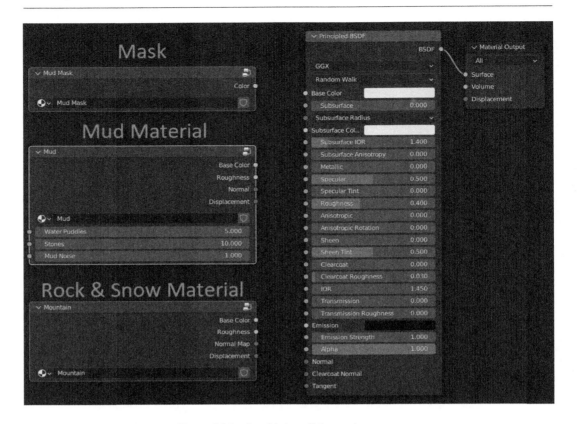

Figure 9.26 – Combining all the node groups

Now let's start by mixing **Base Color**:

1. Bring in a **MixRGB** node.
2. Connect the **Mud Mask** single slot to **Fac** on **MixRGB**.
3. Connect **Mud's Base Color** slot to the **Color1** slot on **MixRGB**.
4. Connect the **Mountain's Base Color** slot to the **Color2** slot of **MixRGB**.
5. Connect **MixRGB's** right-hand **Color** slot to **Principled BSDF's Base Color** slot.

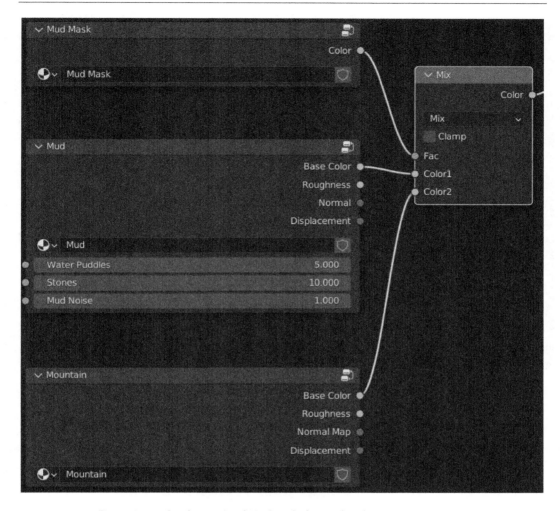

Figure 9.27 – Combining Mud Mask with the Mud and Mountain materials

Let's repeat the same connections we made for the other texturing channels: **Roughness**, **Normal**, and **Displacement**.

Key points:

- **Mask** always needs to be connected to the **Fac** slot of the four **MixRGB** nodes we'll be creating. Check *Figure 9.28*.

- The **Roughness**, **Normal**, and **Displacement** slots on **Mud** need to be connected to **Color1**.

- The **Roughness**, **Normal**, and **Displacement** slots on **Mountain** need to be connected to **Color2**:

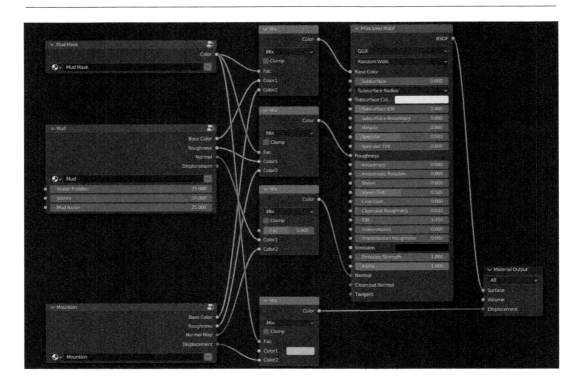

Figure 9.28 – Mixing Mud with Mountain using Mud Mask

And here we are – this is the result of the landscape when texturing it with the rocky snow and mud:

Figure 9.29 – Texturing the landscape with rocky snow and mud

The landscape looks alive with vivid colors! In the next chapter, we will add rocks and grass, and improve the water shader to make it fit the scene better.

Summary

In this chapter, we learned how to texture the landscape by mixing two different materials, rocky snow and mud. We learned how to mix two different materials on the same object while controlling where and to what degree we wanted the mixing to occur by using masks.

Next, we learned how to optimize and organize our node setup by using groups that allow us to simplify a node tree by hiding away complexity.

In the next chapter, we'll be creating assets such as rocks, stones, and grass to enrich our landscape scene.

Part 3: Creating Natural Assets

In the third part of this book, we will focus on creating natural assets to fill our landscape environment. We will start with designing rocks, which are perfect for giving a realistic and natural feeling to our landscape environment. Then, we will learn how to create organic flowers based on real references.

This part includes the following chapters:

- *Chapter 10, Creating Natural Assets: Rock*
- *Chapter 11, Creating Realistic Flowers in Blender*

10
Creating Natural Assets: Rock

In this chapter, we will be creating realistic rock assets using the **Rock Generator** built-in Blender add-on. These rock assets are perfect for giving a realistic and natural feel to the landscape environment we're creating and can be used in multiple exterior nature visualizations.

You will learn how to generate realistic rocks with one click. Also, you will be able to adjust the rocks' shape and add more detail to them.

Next, you'll learn how to unwrap and texture a rock. Here, you will learn the fastest way to set up **PBR (Physically based rendering)** materials in Blender. And finally, you'll learn how to optimize the rock geometry – you'll save 75% of rock geometry without sacrificing too much rock quality.

In this chapter, we'll be covering the following topics:

- Installing the rock generator add-on
- Creating rocks using the rock generator add-on

Technical requirements

This chapter requires a Mac or PC capable of running Blender Version 3.0 or above.

You can download the resources for this chapter from GitHub at `https://github.com/PacktPublishing/3D-Environment-Design-with-Blender/tree/main/chapter-10`

Installing the rock generator add-on

The first step to creating rocks is to enable a pre-installed add-on called rock generator. It's a part of a larger add-on called **Add Mesh: Extra Objects**.

Let's jump into a new Blender scene. At the top, you'll find the **Edit** tab. Click on it and go to **Preferences**:

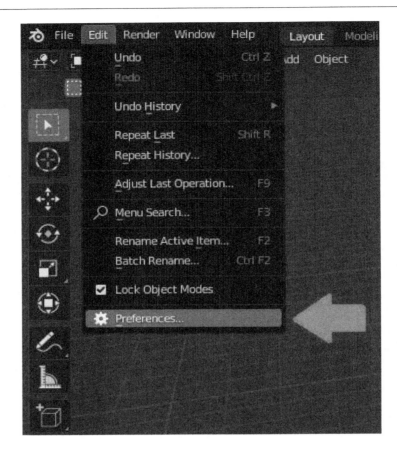

Figure 10.1 – Clicking on Preferences from the Edit menu

A new window will pop up. On the left side, click on **Add-ons** and search for Add Mesh: Extra Objects.

The add-on will be shown in the search results. Click on the left box next to the add-on's name to have the add-on enabled.

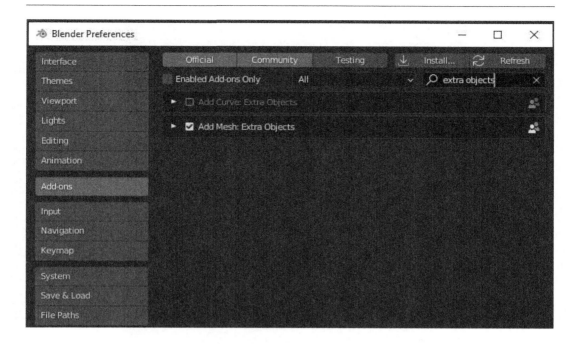

Figure 10.2 – Searching for the Add Mesh: Extra Objects add-on

Basically, that's it – our add-on is installed. We can now use it to add rock objects to our scene.

Creating rocks using the rock generator add-on

To create rocks using the rock generator, let's jump into the 3D Viewport and perform these actions:

1. Press *Shift + A*.

2. Go to **Mesh** and you will find **Rock Generator**.

This add-on also comes with many tools, such as **Gears**, **Pipe Joints**, and so much other stuff. For the scope of this chapter, we'll be focusing only on rocks.

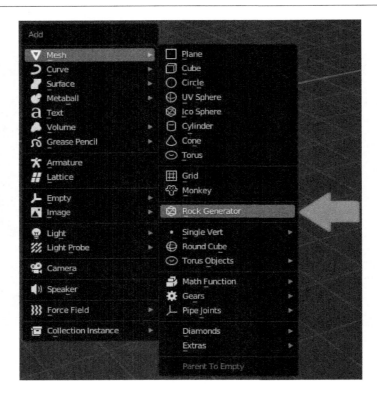

Figure 10.3 – Adding the Rock Generator in the 3D Viewport

Once you click on **Rock Generator**, a rock will appear in your scene. At the bottom left, you'll find a tab called **Add Rocks**. Click on it to start the customization of the rock.

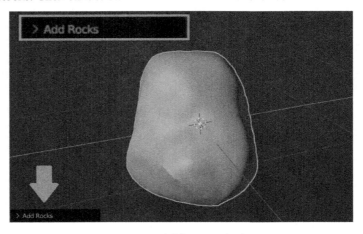

Figure 10.4 – Adding a rock object

Click on the left arrow to expand the panel and access the rock generator settings.

The first thing to do is to disable the **Use a random seed** feature. This feature randomizes the shape of the rock automatically. When you change the **Deformation** value, it keeps generating different new shapes randomly. Personally, I find it frustrating.

The current shape of the rock is boring. The way to generate different rocks is by changing the **User seed** value. In my case, I set it to 7 and it gives me an excellent rock shape to start with. Every time you change the **User seed** value, you generate a different rock shape.

Next, we need to change the **Deformation** value and set it to 10. This will magnify the shape of the rock and make its edges pop out:

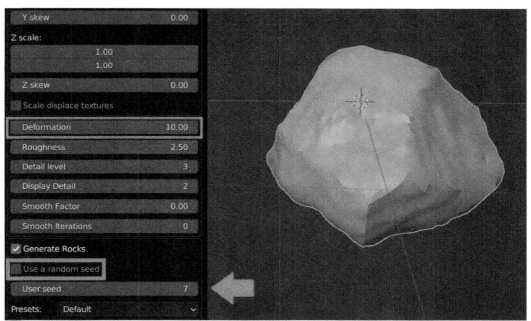

Figure 10.5 – Customizing the shape of the rock object

The way the rock generator add-on works is by adding multiple modifiers to the rock object, such as **Subdivision Surface** and **Displace** modifiers. We'll see that later when we optimize the rock.

To give the rock more details, let's add a new **Subdivision Surface** modifier. In **Modifier Properties**, you will find a bunch of modifiers added to our rock. The new modifier will be added as the last modifier in the list.

Set the **Levels Viewport** value to 1 and the same for **Render**. Don't exceed 1 for **Levels Viewport** as making the value higher will directly affect the performance.

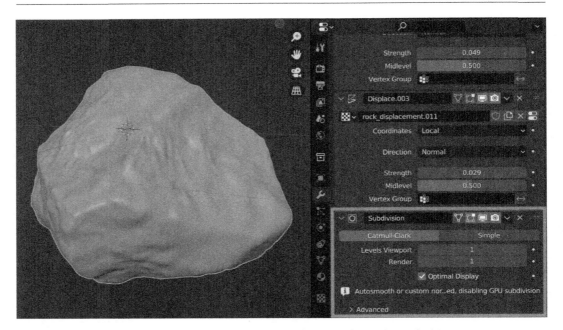

Figure 10.6 – Adding a Subdivision Surface modifier to the rock object

The shape of our rock is perfect now. Let's proceed with texturing it.

Texturing the rock

In order to texture the rock, we'll be using a rock PBR texture, which you can download using this link: `https://github.com/PacktPublishing/3D-Environment-Design-with-Blender/blob/main/chapter-10/Rock-PBR-Texture.zip`.

Let's get started with creating a material and assign it to our rock.

Creating a rock material

To create the rock material, let's select the rock object and go to **Material Properties**, add a new material, and call it `Rock`.

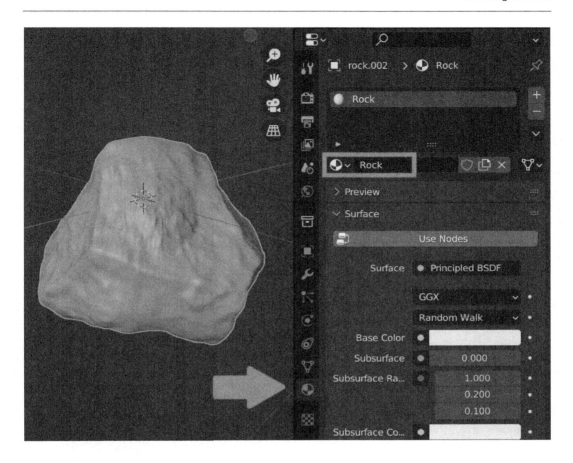

Figure 10.7 – Adding a Rock material to the rock object

In order to edit the **Rock** material, and switch the bottom window of your Blender scene to **Shader Editor**. By default, the **Rock** material will have two nodes: **Principled BSDF** and **Material Output**.

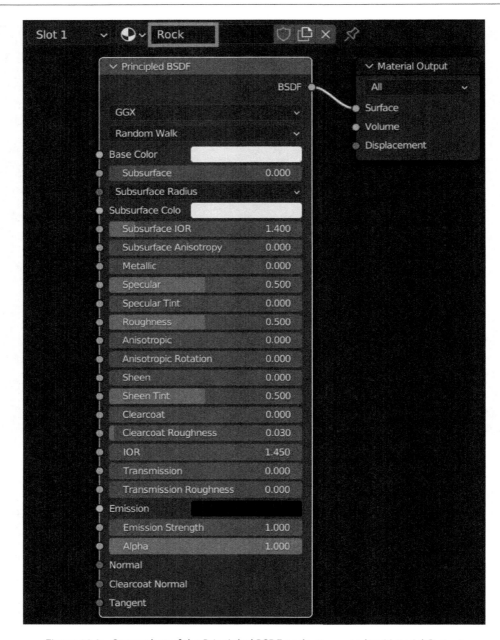

Figure 10.8 – Screenshot of the Principled BSDF node connected to Material Output

Our next move is to assign rock textures to the rock object. To achieve this, we'll use a trick that allows us to set up PBR materials with one click.

The fastest way to set up PBR materials in Blender

Creating materials using nodes it's perhaps one of the most daunting tasks for a 3D artist. It's repetitive, boring, and time-consuming. But fortunately, there is an add-on that makes working with nodes much easier, and that is the Node Wrangler.

The Node Wrangler is a built-in add-on in Blender that has multiple features. In this part of the book, we'll be using this add-on to assign PBR textures the fastest way. Let's make sure it's installed first:

1. Go to the **Edit** tab from the top menu of your Blender scene.

2. Choose **Preferences**, which is the last tab in the list.

Figure 10.9 – Clicking on Preferences from the Edit menu

3. A new window will pop up. Go to the **Add-ons** tab from the left menu.

4. You will find a search box at the top right.

5. Search for Node Wrangler.

6. The add-on will appear in the list. Make sure to check the box to have the add-on activated.

Figure 10.10 – Searching for the Node Wrangler add-on

Now the **Node Wrangler** add-on is enabled and we can use it to assign rock textures to our rock object. To do that, let's go back to the Shader Editor and follow these steps:

1. Click on the **Principled BSDF** node to have it highlighted. This node will serve as the base for the PBR rock texture maps.

2. Press *Ctrl + Shift + T* and a new file browser window will pop up.

3. Locate the texture maps that you want to import from the rock folder you downloaded before and click on the bottom **Principled Texture Setup** button.

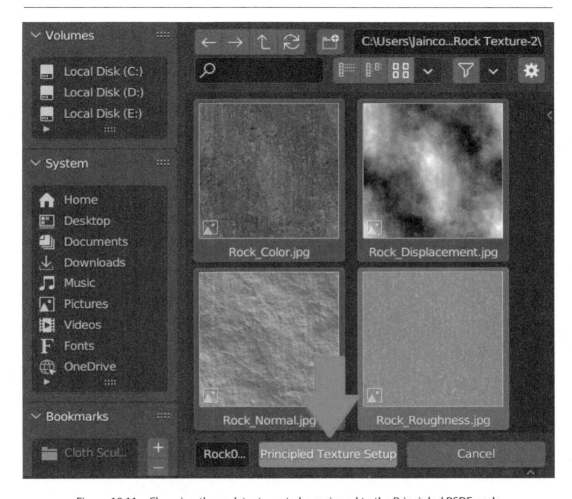

Figure 10.11 – Choosing the rock textures to be assigned to the Principled BSDF node

By using the combination of *Ctrl + Shift + T*, you will have all the textures assigned automatically as nodes to **Principled BSDF** with just a single click. You will also have the **Mapping** node on the left side, allowing you to adjust the scale and position of the rock texture.

To understand how the add-on works, it simply searched for keywords related to the names of these textures. If the add-on finds the word `Color` in the name of a texture, it assigns that `Color` texture to **Base Color** of **Principled BSDF**. This is why you need to make sure that the texture map names are clear.

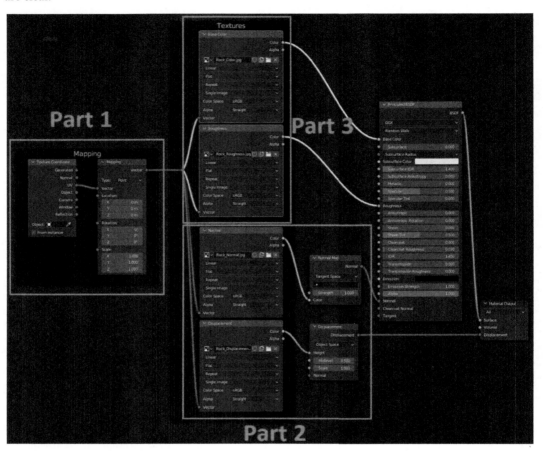

Figure 10.12 – Rock material node setup

This is Part 1 of our node setup. Here, the **Node Wrangler** add-on adds two nodes:

- **Texture Coordinate**

- **Mapping**

These two nodes will allow us to manipulate the scale and rotation of our texture image.

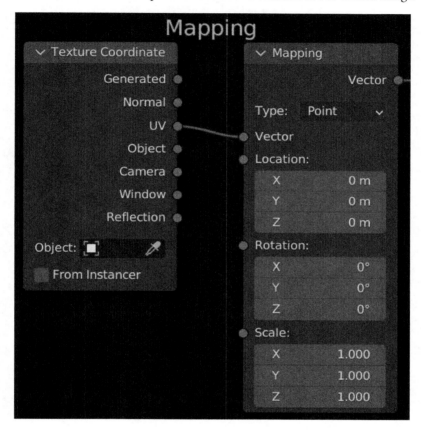

Figure 10.13 – Part 1 of the rock material node setup

In Part 2, we have the **Normal** map assigned to **Normal Map** and then assigned to the **Normal** slot of **Principled BSDF**, and the **Displacement** texture assigned to the **Displacement** node and then assigned to the **Material Output Displacement** slot.

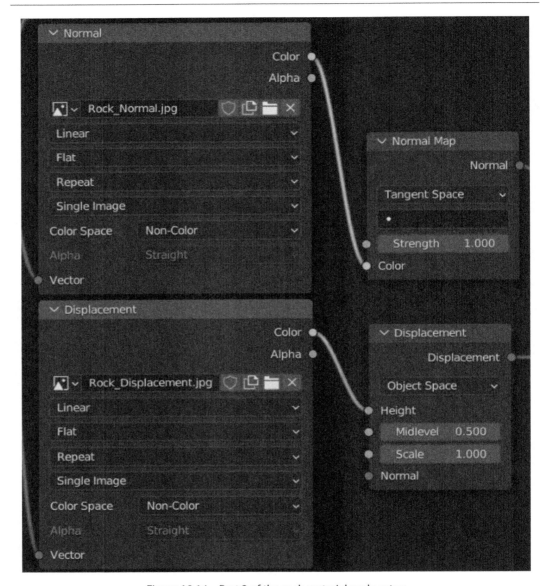

Figure 10.14 – Part 2 of the rock material node setup

In Part 3 of our node setup, we have the **Color** texture assigned to the **Base Color** slot of **Principled BSDF** and **Roughness** assigned to the **Roughness** channel in **Principled BSDF**.

Figure 10.15 – Part 3 of the rock material node setup

Now, if we switch to **Material Preview** by pressing *Z* in the 3D Viewport, this is how our rock will appear:

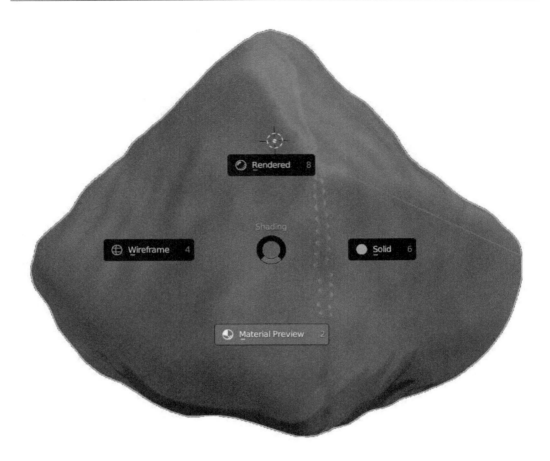

Figure 10.16 – Displaying the non-unwrapped rock in Material Preview

We're not able to see the rock texture on our rock because the rock object is not unwrapped yet. Let's go ahead and unwrap our rock object.

Unwrapping the rock object

In order to unwrap our rock and have it ready to be textured, let's perform these actions:

1.   Select the rock object first.

2.   Switch to **Edit** mode by pressing *Tab*.

3.   Press *U* and choose **Cube Projection**.

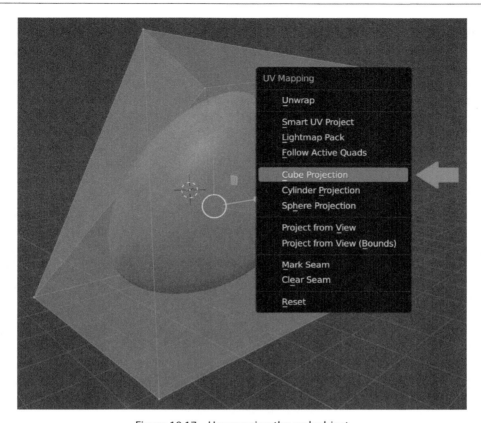

Figure 10.17 – Unwrapping the rock object

Now, if we switch to **Material Preview**, our rock will be unwrapped and well textured.

Figure 10.18 – Displaying the unwrapped rock in Material Preview

But we need to see our rock in **Rendered** mode, to have a better idea of how it will appear in our final rendered scene. So, let's do a quick lighting setup in our scene.

Setting up quick lighting for our scene

In order to better see our rock, let's set up a quick lighting setup for our scene. In the Shader Editor, switch the data type to **World**.

Add a new **Sky Texture** node and connect it to the **Background** node.

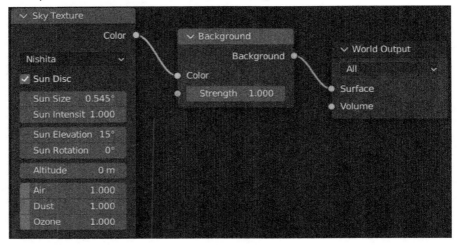

Figure 10.19 – Setting up the Sky Texture lighting node

To use the **Sky Texture node**, always make sure that you are on the **Cycles** render engine. You can check that out by going to **Render Properties** in the right panel.

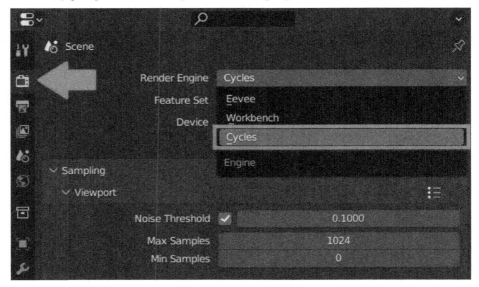

Figure 10.20 – Switching Render Engine to Cycles

Let's go ahead and switch the **preview mode** to **Rendered**. This is how our rock looks:

Figure 10.21 – Displaying the rock in Rendered Preview

We can make our rock better by using the **Displacement** texture because it's not being used right now. To activate it, let's go to **Material Properties**, select our **Rock** material, and scroll down to **Displacement**.

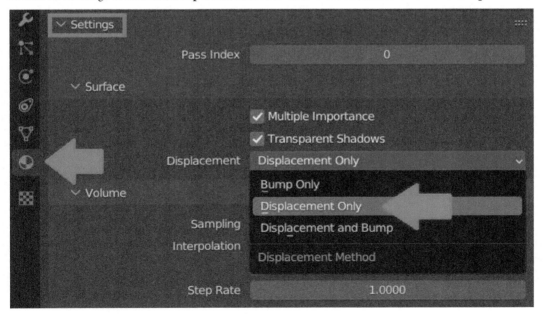

Figure 10.22 – Switching the Displacement setting to Displacement Only

Now, if we switch to the **rendered** mode again, our rock will explode like this:

Figure 10.23 – Rock object with the displacement scale set to 1

To get the rock shape right, let's reduce the **Scale** value of the **Displacement** node in the **Shader Editor** to **0.100**, as follows:

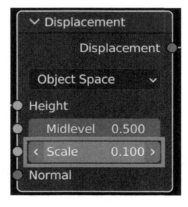

Figure 10.24 – Reducing the scale of the rock material Displacement to 0.100

This is how the rock will look. Much better, huh? Now we can say that our rock rocks.

Note

Keep in mind that the **Scale** value is relative to the rock's scale. If we scale up the rock 10 times, we should also increase **Scale** of **Displacement** to 1 instead of 0.100.

Figure 10.25 – Rock object with Displacement Scale set to 0.100

The last step to do is to apply some optimization to our rock. It's heavy in geometry right now. We need to reduce the number of vertices that the rock holds because we'll be duplicating this rock tens of times in our landscape scene.

Optimizing the rock geometry

Before we can optimize the rock geometry, let's enable **Statistics** in **Show Overlays**.

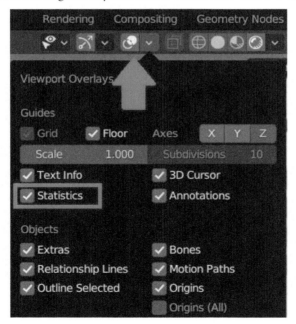

Figure 10.26 – Activating Statistics in Show Overlays

This way, if we select an object in our scene, we will be able to see its statistics on the right side of the Blender scene. In this example, we've selected the rock object and it says that it has more than 12,000 vertices.

Figure 10.27 – Displaying the rock object statistics

In order to reduce the number of vertices in our rock, let's go to **Modifier Properties**.

You will find a bunch of modifiers added by the Rock Generator. The first two modifiers are **Subdivision Surface** modifiers:

1. Let's reduce the **Levels Viewport** value of the first **Subdivision Surface** modifier to 1, as well as **Render**.

2. For the second **Subdivision Surface modifier**, let's keep the **Levels Viewport** value at 2, as well as **Render**.

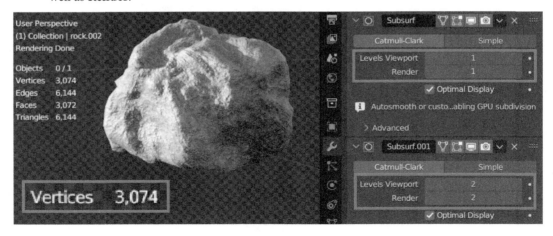

Figure 10.28 – Optimizing the rock object

Immediately, we dropped the number of vertices from over 12,000 to around 3,000, without sacrificing too much quality.

That's a huge drop. Imagine that we need to duplicate our rock 50 times in the landscape scene.

With our non-optimized rock, it would cost us around 600,000 vertices (12,000 * 50). That's more than half a million vertices for rocks only. But with our optimized rock, it will cost us only 150,000 vertices.

Summary

In this chapter, we went through the process of creating realistic rock assets using the Rock Generator built-in Blender add-on. We learned how to generate and adjust the shape of rocks with one click.

Then, we learned how to unwrap and texture the rock using the **Node Wrangler** add-on. And finally, we optimized the rock's geometry, saving 75% of the rock geometry without sacrificing too much rock quality.

In the next chapter, we'll be creating a new natural asset, which is flowers. Both rocks and flowers will be used to populate our landscape scene, making it look natural and realistic.

11
Creating Realistic Flowers in Blender

In this chapter, you will learn tips on how to create an organic-looking flower in Blender for our landscape environment scene. The flower that we'll be creating will be based on a real reference – the name of the flower is buttercup.

We will start by modeling the petals and the center. We will use the **Displace** modifier to add cloud noise to the surface of the petals.

Next, we will learn how to unwrap and texture the buttercup flower. Finally, we will diversify the flower branches, add the leaves using the alpha transparency trick, and give the flower a realistic scale measurement.

In this chapter, we'll be covering the following topics:

- Designing buttercup petals
- Texturing the buttercup
- Creating the buttercup leaves
- Sizing the buttercup flower

Technical requirements

This chapter requires a Mac or PC capable of running Blender Version 3.0 or above.

You can download the resources for this chapter from GitHub at `https://github.com/PacktPublishing/3D-Environment-Design-with-Blender/tree/main/chapter-11`

Designing a buttercup

Let's start by creating the buttercup petals. Since this is a real flower, we must use a real reference in order to make the final result accurate. We'll be using this image reference of a buttercup flower:

Figure 11.1 – Buttercup flower petals

You can download this buttercup flower image reference from this link: `https://github.com/PacktPublishing/3D-Environment-Design-with-Blender/blob/main/chapter-11/Flower-Petals.jpg`

After downloading this reference, press *7* while on the 3D Viewport to go to the **Top Orthographic** view and simply drag and drop this reference image into the 3D Viewport:

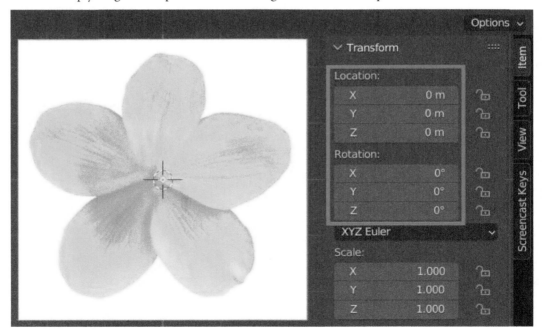

Figure 11.2 – Dragging the flower reference in the 3D Viewport

This way, we'll have the image reference laid out. Press *N* to access the **Transform** panel and make sure that the **Location** and **Rotation** values are set to 0 so that we can put the flower reference in the center of the grid.

Modeling the buttercup flower petals

Let's start by creating a plane mesh and putting it on one of the petals in our reference:

1. In **Edit Mode**, press *Ctrl + E* and choose **Subdivide**. This way, we'll subdivide our plane into four different small faces. We do this to have a sufficient number of vertices on the edge of the plane to control.

2. Make sure to also switch the preview mode to **Wireframe** by pressing *Z* in the 3D Viewport so that we can see the flower reference and follow its petal edges.

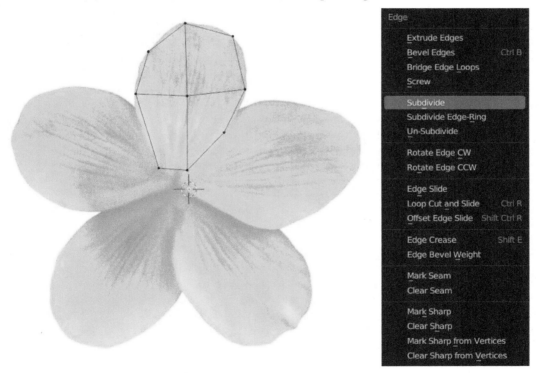

Figure 11.3 – Subdividing the plane using the Ctrl + E hotkey

Next, we'll need to add the **Subdivision Surface** modifier to the plane to make the petal smooth. See the following:

Figure 11.4 – Adding the Subdivision Surface modifier to the plane

3.   Next, let's repeat the same alignment steps for the other petals – you can just duplicate the same plane, spin it, and put it on the next petal. Once you have finished with the alignment of the petals, our flower creation progress should look like this:

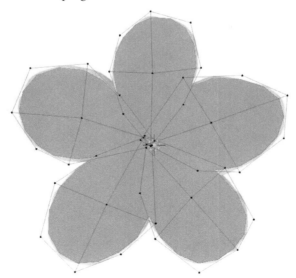

Figure 11.5 – Aligning the planes with the petals

Now, we need to create the petals' curvature. So far, the petals are flat, and we need to bend them upward. Let's only select the outer vertices of all five petals and lift them until curvature is created:

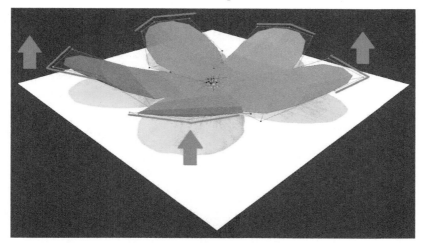

Figure 11.6 – Moving the petal edges of the flower up

To have a better idea of how buttercup petals look, let's take a look at a real image of this flower:

Figure 11.7 – Real reference of the buttercup flower

You can see that the surface of the petals is not smooth, so we need to add some noisy bumps to the surface. To accomplish that, we'll be using the **Displace** modifier:

1. Select the petal object in **Object** mode.
2. Go to **Texture Properties**.

3. Click on **New** to add a new texture.

4. Set the new texture type to **Clouds**:

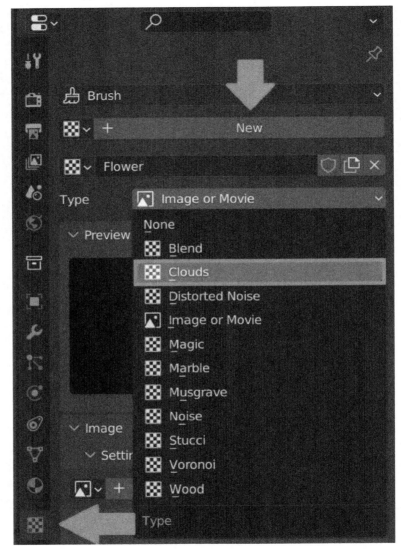

Figure 11.8 – Adding the Clouds texture

5. Go to **Modifier Properties** and search for the **Displace** modifier.

6. In the texture field highlighted in the green box in the following figure choose the **Flower** texture we created:

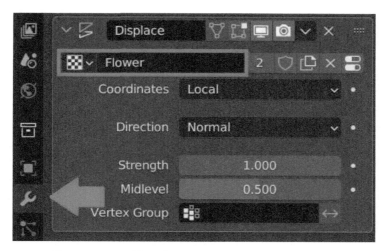

Figure 11.9 – Adding the Displace modifier to the flower

With the **Displace** modifier set to **Clouds**, the shape of the flower will look like this:

Figure 11.10 – Showing the flower with the Displace modifier applied

Its edges look pointy and sharp, but we can fix that by adding another **Subdivision Surface** modifier, similar to what we did in *Figure 11.4*. This is the new look of our petals:

Figure 11.11 – Smoothing the flower petals by adding a Subdivision Surface modifier

Now that we have the flower petals, let's go ahead and create the stem of our buttercup flower.

Modeling the buttercup flower stem

The stem is the main long and thin green part of a plant that rises above the soil and supports the buttercup flower:

Figure 11.12 – Reference of the buttercup flower

To create the flower stem, let's add a cube, jump into **Edit Mode**, and follow these steps:

1. Insert four horizontal edge loops.

2. Select each edge loop using *Alt + left-mouse click* and scale each edge loop as shown in the middle of the following figure.

3. Add a **Subdivision Surface** modifier to this object.

4. Right-click and choose **Shade Smooth** to smooth the stem shape.

5. Bring back the petals and place them in the center of our stem as shown here:

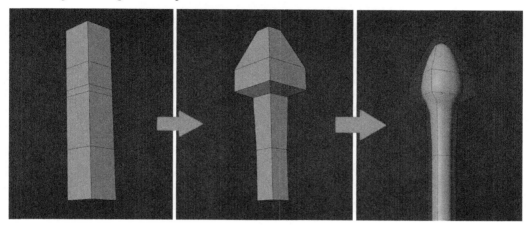

Figure 11.13 – Stem creation steps

Let's work on the center of our flower by adding small objects around the center:

1. Add a plane.

2. Scale it down as shown on the left side of *Figure 11.14*.

3. Add the **Subdivision Surface** modifier to the plane.

Duplicate it around the flower stem center.

Figure 11.14 – Inner flower creation

And this is how our flower looks so far:

Figure 11.15 – Displaying the buttercup flower in the Solid mode

Before we can duplicate our flower to make branches out of it, let's finish texturing it first.

Texturing the buttercup flower

Before we can proceed with texturing our flower, we need to make sure that all the petals of the flower are merged into one piece. To do that, you can press *Ctrl + J* to join them all into one unit. Now, let's proceed with texturing the petals:

1.   Select the petals, go to **Material Properties**, add a new material, and call it FlowerLeaves:

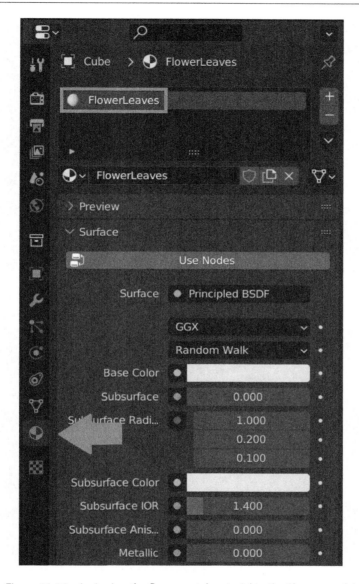

Figure 11.16 – Assigning the flower petal material to the Flower model

2. Switch the bottom window of your Blender scene to **Shader Editor**.

3. Drag the image reference we used earlier into **Shader Editor** and connect it to **Base Color:**

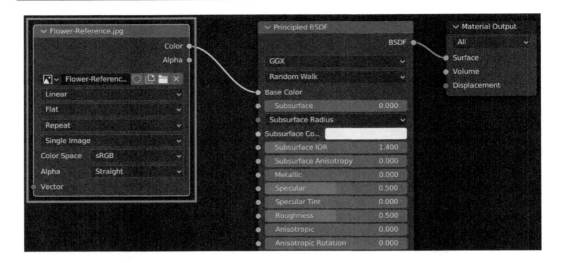

Figure 11.17 – Connecting the texture to Base Color

4.   Now, if we press *Z* and switch to **Material Preview**, this is how our flower will look:

Figure 11.18 – Default unwrapping of the flower

Our flower isn't properly textured because it has bad UVs. That's why we need to improve the flower UVs.

Unwrapping the buttercup flower

We'll be unwrapping our flower by projecting the UVs from the top. To do that, let's perform these actions:

1. Press *7* in the 3D Viewport to go to the top.

2. Switch to **Edit Mode** and press *U* and choose **Project from View (Bounds)**:

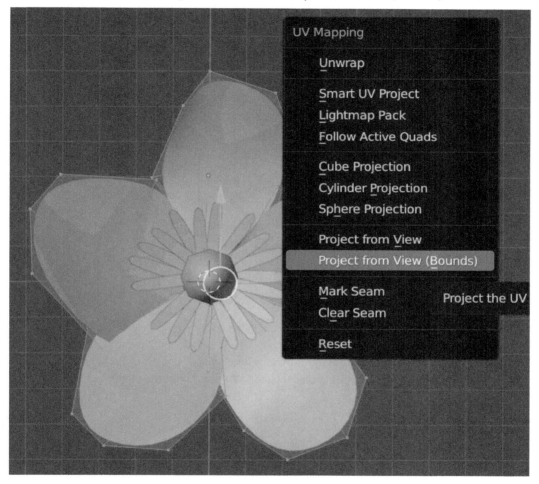

Figure 11.19 – Unwrapping the flower model

3. Switch from **Shader Editor** to **UV Editor** and start aligning the UVs with the reference petals. Do your best – it doesn't need to be 100% perfect.

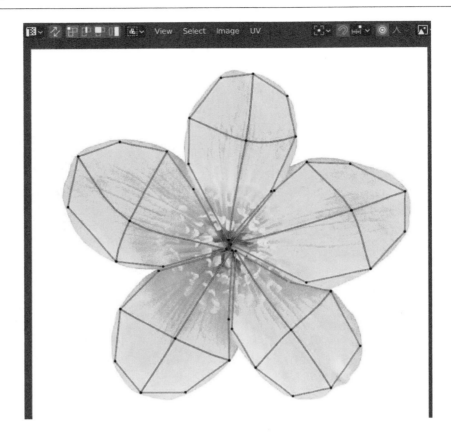

Figure 11.20 – Tweaking the flower UVs

This is how our flower will look – it's better unwrapped but still looks boring. So far, we only worked on the **Base Color** node of our flower. We need to work on the **Roughness** map, as well as **Bump**.

Figure 11.21 – Texturing the flower petals

Let's tweak the other material channels – so back to **Shader Editor**:

1. Connect the **Flower-Reference** texture to a **ColorRamp** node.

2. Move the two **ColorRamp** handles close to each other.

3. Connect the right-hand slot of **ColorRamp** to the **Roughness** channel. This will give our flower petals a nice reflection.

4. Connect the **Flower-Reference** texture to a **Bump** node.

5. Set the **Strength** value of the **Bump** node to `0.15`:

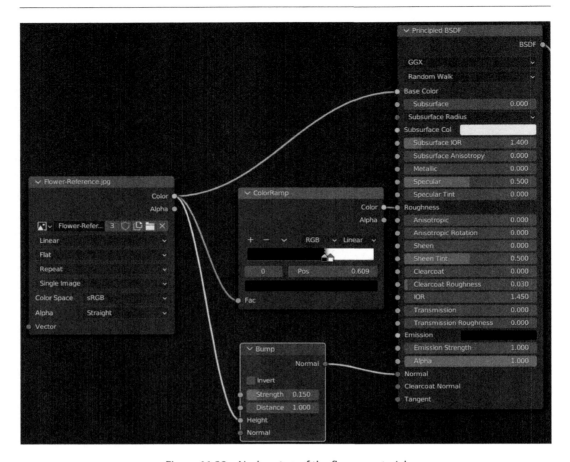

Figure 11.22 – Node setup of the flower material

This will make the petals' reflection appear as in the following figure. Now, I want you to select all the small planes, join them using *Ctrl + J*, and, again, join them to the petals. This way the small inner petals will have the same material and modifiers as those applied to the big, outer petals:

Figure 11.23 – Texturing the buttercup flower

Texturing the buttercup flower stem

Let's create the second green material for the center stem. To do, that let's perform these actions:

1. Select the center stem and add a new material to it called Green Stem.

2. In **Shader Editor**, add **Musgrave Texture**:

    I.   Set **Scale** to 25

    II.   Set **Detail** to 15

    III.   Increase **Dimension** to 7.5

3. Connect **Musgrave Texture** to a **ColorRamp** node:

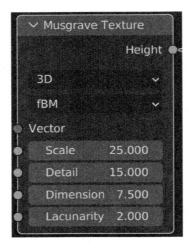

Figure 11.24 – The Musgrave Texture node

4. Set the colors of the two handles to different green colors in the **ColorRamp** node:

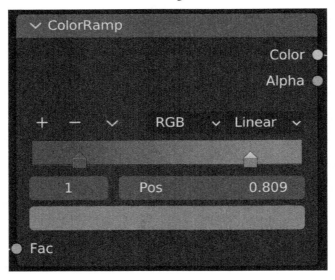

Figure 11.25 – The ColorRamp node

5. Connect **Musgrave Texture** to the **Bump** node and connect **Bump** to the **Normal** slot on **Principled BSDF**.

6. Set the **Strength** value of **Bump** to 0.25:

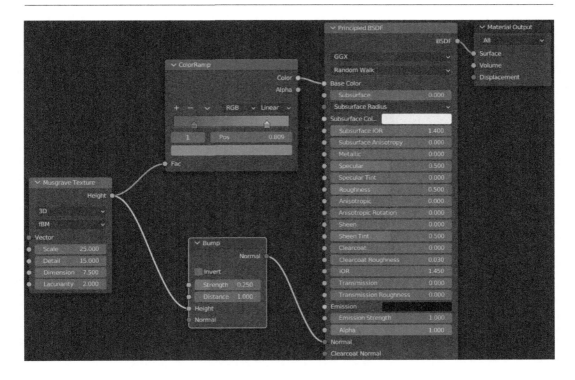

Figure 11.26 – Stem node setup material

This is what our flower looks like:

Figure 11.27 – Finishing the texturing of the buttercup flower

Now, we need to diversify our flower by branching it out multiple times. You can do that by duplicating the first flower and attaching it to the same stem, while giving it a different orientation. Make sure that the main stem is thicker than the secondary stem.

Figure 11.28 – Second level branching of the buttercup flower

After duplicating a few branches, this is how our flower will look:

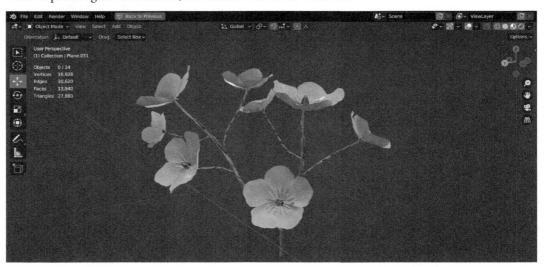

Figure 11.29 – Branching the buttercup flower

Now we have created the buttercup flower and textured it. There is still a missing element to our flower to be finished, which is the buttercup leaves, so let's create them.

Creating the buttercup leaves

The next step is to create the buttercup flower leaves. Based on this reference, we can see the shape of a buttercup's leaves:

Figure 11.30 – Image reference of buttercup flower leaves

You can download this leaf image reference from this link: `https://github.com/PacktPublishing/3D-Environment-Design-with-Blender/blob/main/chapter-11/Leaf-Texture.jpg`.

Let's go ahead and create the buttercup flower leaves.

Applying textures with Alpha transparency

To create the flower leaves using the Alpha transparency trick, let's follow these steps:

1. Create a plane.
2. Assign a new material called `Leaf` to the plane.
3. Drop the leaf image you have downloaded into **Shader Editor** and connect it to **Base Color**:

Figure 11.31 – Texturing the buttercup flower leaves

4. Insert a couple of edge loops and change the shape of the plane to this:

Figure 11.32 – Changing the shape of the plane to fit the leaves

5. Download this leaf texture, drop it into **Shader Editor**, and assign it to the plane.

When rendering this plane, all we need to show is the leaf – the other white spots must be transparent. This is where the **Alpha** slot on **Principled BSDF** comes into play. We need to create a black and white texture out of the leaf texture, with white representing the green leaf and black representing the leaf surroundings.

To do that, let's perform these steps:

1. Connect the **Color** slot of the leaf texture to the **Fac** slot of the **ColorRamp** node.
2. Connect the **Color** slot of **ColorRamp** to the **Alpha** slot of **Principled BSDF**.
3. Switch the **ColorRamp** type to **Constant** to give sharper edges to the leaf.

Connect the **Color** slot of the **Leaf** texture to the **Base Color** slot on **Principled BSDF**:

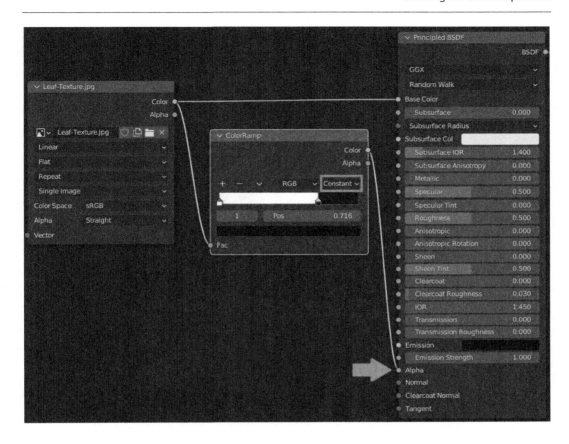

Figure 11.33 – Leaf node setup material

4. When connecting **Leaf-Texture** to **ColorRamp**, the **ColorRamp** node will convert the leaf texture into a black-and-white texture (grayscale), as shown here:

Figure 11.34 – Black and white leaf mask

When connecting this texture to the **Alpha** slot on **Principled BSDF**, Blender will only display what is white and make the black areas transparent when rendering:

Figure 11.35 – Making the leaf texture transparent on the edges

To make the leaf look better, make sure to work on **Roughness** and add bumps, similar to what we did in *Figure 11.22*.

Put the leaves in different places on the flower, as seen here:

Figure 11.36 – Buttercup flower final result in Material Preview

Our buttercup flower shape is now finished – the last thing to make sure of is the scale of our flower. We need to give it a proper, realistic scale, so let's do that.

Sizing the buttercup flower

Our last step is to give the flower the right measurements. Based on Google research, buttercups reach 31 cm in height, so any size in height between 20 cm and 30 cm will look reasonable.

In our example, the longest stem height is 0.27 m, so we can say that our flower branch size is reasonable. In case you have a different size, you can press *N* to access the right-hand **Transform** panel, select all the flower elements, and scale them up or down until they reach a realistic size.

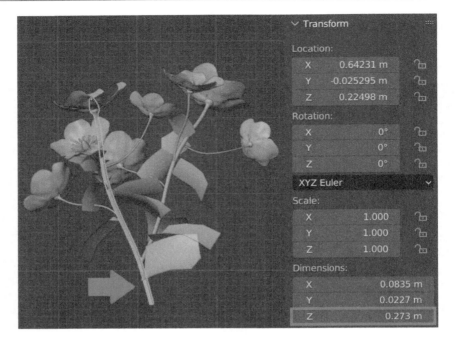

Figure 11.37 – Measuring the buttercup flower main stem

Now that our flower is complete and well-sized, let's take a look at how our flower will look in the **Render** mode.

To make sure it looks good when imported into our landscape scene, this is how our buttercup flower will look when finally rendered:

Figure 11.38 – Final render of the buttercup flower

I did the following:

1. I set up HDRI lighting.
2. I added a camera and made it focus on the flowers.
3. I used **Depth of Field** to blur the flowers in the background.

We will learn how to do all of that in the final chapter of this book.

Summary

We've 3D-designed a beautiful buttercup flower. We started by 3D modeling the buttercup petals, and basically, we kept on modifying the shape of the petals based on real references. We used the **Displace** modifier to add a **Clouds** noise to the surface of the petals.

The next step was unwrapping and texturing the buttercup flower.

Finally, we diversified the flower branches by creating the flower once and then copying and modifying it as per our requirements.

We used the alpha transparency trick to add the leaves to the buttercup flower stem.

In the next chapter, we will learn how to use the **Particle System** options to scatter flowers and rocks all over our landscape environment.

Part 4: Rendering Epic Landscape Shots

In the last part of this book, we'll be learning about the Blender Particle System to scatter all the natural assets we created. Then, we will finalize and apply some improvements and final touches to the landscape environment. Finally, we will learn about rendering and compositing to create epic landscape shots.

This part includes the following chapters:

- *Chapter 12, Using Particle System to Scatter Objects in Blender*
- *Chapter 13, Finalizing the Landscape Scene – Lighting, Rendering, and Compositing*

Using Particle System to Scatter Objects in Blender

In this chapter, we will use **Particle System** in Blender to scatter flowers and rocks throughout our landscape environment. First, we will understand what the **Particle System** option in Blender is and why you should use it.

Next, we will learn how to add and place particles in a specific chosen area and change the scale and rotation of particles while controlling their quantity.

Finally, we will learn a trick to boost the performance of Blender while dealing with particles.

In this chapter, we'll be covering the following topics:

- What is **Particle System** in Blender?
- Importing rock and flower assets into the landscape environment

Technical requirements

This chapter requires a Mac or PC capable of running Blender Version 3.0 or above.

You can download the resources for this chapter from GitHub at `https://github.com/PacktPublishing/3D-Environment-Design-with-Blender/tree/main/chapter-12`

What is Particle System in Blender?

Particle systems are used to simulate large amounts of small moving objects, creating fire, dust, clouds, smoke, fur, grass, and other strand-based materials.

As of Blender 3.3, there are two types of Particle System configurations: **Emitter** and **Hair**. In this chapter, we'll be focusing on the second type – which is **Hair**. The most common use of the **Hair** type of **Particle System** in Blender is to scatter objects across a surface.

Why should I use the Hair type of Particle System?

You might wonder why you should bother learning about this particle system stuff, which potentially seems intimidating from its name. I will show you why.

You can proceed without learning about this particle system thing, but let me tell you, this is the difference between hard and smart work. A task that could take up to 2 hours of hard work can be achieved in 10 minutes using particles with ease.

I want you to consider this situation – your project is to build a 3D garden in Blender. You have created all the assets in your garden: plants, flowers, rocks, and stones. Now, it's time to scatter all these assets across different areas of your garden, but there are some tips to keep in mind:

- The size of plants should be different. As you know, in nature, it's almost impossible to find two plants of 100% the same size. The same thing goes for the orientation of plants – each plant must have a different rotation angle on all angles, X, Y, and Z.

- The plants should be scattered randomly – there shouldn't be an obvious pattern:

Figure 12.1 – Good example of a particle system used to scatter plants across a sphere object

With the **Hair** particle system, you can determine where to put your assets, randomize their scale and rotation, and change their position on a map in just a few clicks. Let's use the particle system to scatter rocks and flowers across our landscape scene, but first, we need to import them into the scene.

Importing rock and flower assets into the landscape environment

The first thing we need to do is to import the rock and flower objects into the landscape scene, so let's go back to the landscape scene from *Chapter 9, Texturing the Landscape with Mud Material*. In this scene, we have the landscape textured with rocky snow and mud.

Figure 12.2 – Final result of the landscape scene from Chapter 9

Let's import the **Rock** object into our landscape scene.

Importing the Rock object

To import the **Rock** object that we created in *Chapter 10, Creating Natural Assets: Rock*, let's perform these actions:

1. Go to **File** and click on **Append**:

Figure 12.3 – Choosing Append from the File menu

2.   Choose the **Rocks** Blender file and click on it:

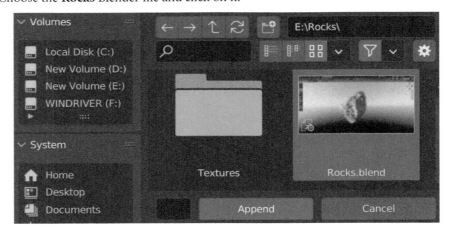

Figure 12.4 – Clicking on the Rocks Blender file

3.   Click on the **Object** folder:

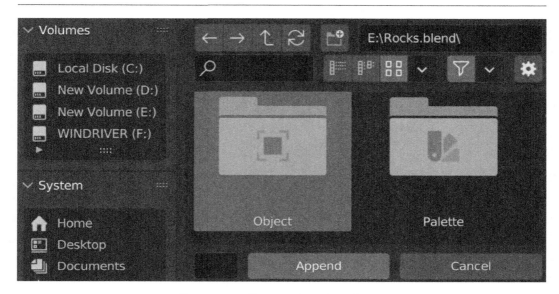

Figure 12.5 – Choosing the Object folder

4.   Double-click on the **Rock** object:

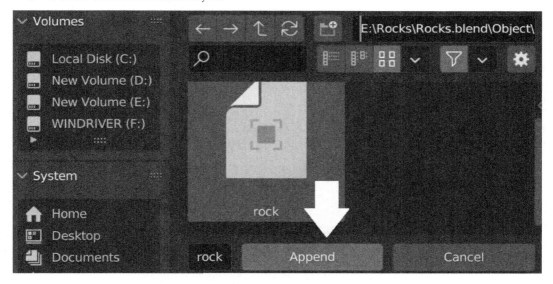

Figure 12.6 – Choosing the Rock object to be appended

And basically, you'll have the rock in your scene:

Figure 12.7 – The Rock object appended to the scene

The next step is to append the flowers to our scene. Repeat the same steps with this flower library that you can download here: https://github.com/PacktPublishing/3D-Environment-Design-with-Blender/blob/a15652a3e7b406a7c70cd8b63837922aea6b151b/chapter-12/Flowers-Collection.zip.

Now that we have both the rocks and flowers, let's proceed by scattering them in our landscape environment.

Using particles to scatter rocks in the landscape environment

In the **Properties** window on the right, below the **Modifier Properties** tab, we have the **Particle Properties** tab. You can see the icon looks like an object shooting particles out from its main body.

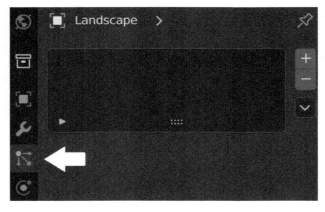

Figure 12.8 – Accessing the Particle Properties tab

Here, you can create particle systems and add them to the object you have selected by clicking on the plus symbol on the right.

By default, the **Particle System** type added to our landscape object will be **Emitter**, and as explained before, we will be using the other type, which is **Hair**.

Next, we need to check the **Advanced** checkbox so that we have access to the full physics calculations that Blender offers with particles.

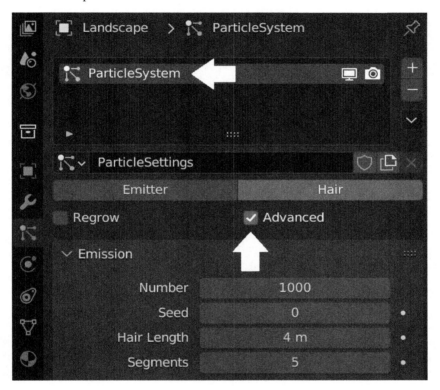

Figure 12.9 – Adding Rocks Particles

Since we'll be creating more than one particle system, we need to change the name of our new particle system to something recognizable such as Rocks Particles so that we can make it easy to customize.

Now, if you pay close attention to your landscape, you will find weird hair particles appearing on the surface of your landscape. Basically, we have 1,000 particles scattered all over the landscape:

Figure 12.10 – Displaying particles in the landscape environment

But how can we control where we want the particles to appear – in different words, where we want the rocks to be?

Placing the particles in the landscape

We need to determine the area in which we want to disperse the rocks.

The easy way to determine where to place particles is by creating a vertex group using **Object Data Properties**. To do that, let's proceed with these steps:

1. Select the landscape and go to **Edit Mode**.
2. Select the faces on the water edge:

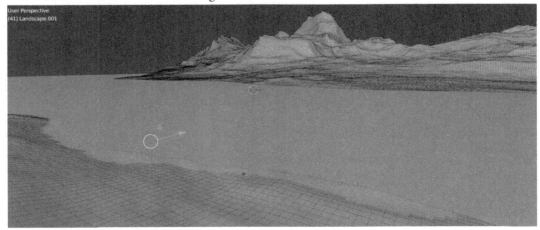

Figure 12.11 – Selecting the area where to display particles

> **Note**
>
> To avoid performance problems such as lagging and Blender crashing, we need to only select a small area for our rock particles. The greater the vertex you select in your landscape, the more resources your computer will need.

Take note – focus only on developing what's in front of your camera because that's what's going to be in your final render.

Once you select the area where you want the rocks to be, go to **Object Data Properties** and perform these actions:

1. Click on the plus symbol to add a new vertex group, and name it `Rocks`.
2. Click **Assign** to assign the selected faces to the **Rocks** vertex group:

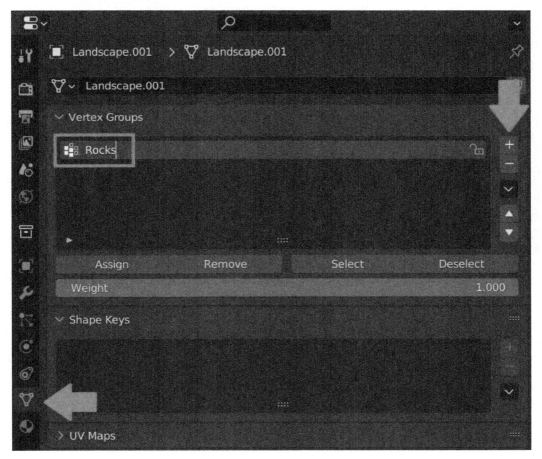

Figure 12.12 – Assigning the Rocks vertices in Vertex Groups

Now the selected vertices of our landscape are saved in the **Rocks** vertex group. To use them, let's go back to the **Particle System** settings:

1. Scroll down to **Vertex Groups**.

2. Click on the **Density** tab, and you'll find the **Rocks** vertex group we created:

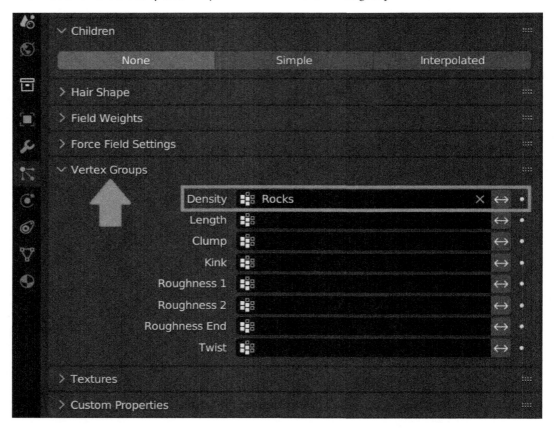

Figure 12.13 – Assigning Density to the Rocks vertex group

Now, if we take a look at our landscape, we will find that the particles are concentrated in this **Rocks** vertex group:

Figure 12.14 – Displaying particles in the Rocks vertex group area

Using Weight Paint to distribute particles

Weight Paint is a brush that allows us to create a heatmap on an object with vertices. The heat map is a cold-to-hot color gradient – blue (cold) refers to no distribution of particles, while red means 100% distribution of particles in the red area.

This is an example of a heatmap:

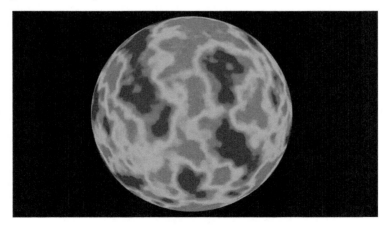

Figure 12.15 – Example of a heatmap

Weight painting gives us an advanced way to spread particles – now, we can control how many particles we want to have in a particular area by setting the **Weight** value.

Let's use **Weight Paint** to spread the particles better:

1. Select the landscape object.

2. Switch **Object Mode** to **Weight Paint**:

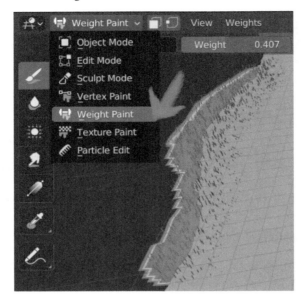

Figure 12.16 – Switching from Object Mode to Weight Paint

You will see the vertex group we assigned earlier highlighted in red. You will also notice that the cursor is replaced by a small red circle, which is the **Weight Paint** brush.

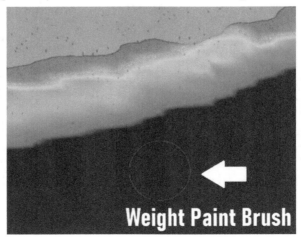

Figure 12.17 – Image showing the Weight Paint brush

3. If you right-click on the landscape, you will have access to three settings to change:

    • **Weight**: This option allows you to change the color of the brush from blue (value of 0.000) to red (value of 1.000). If you paint an area red, the density of hair particles will be high. Painting in blue makes the painted area low in density.

    • **Radius**: This option changes the size of the brush's weight.

    • **Strength**: This determines how powerful the weight paint brush is when applied.

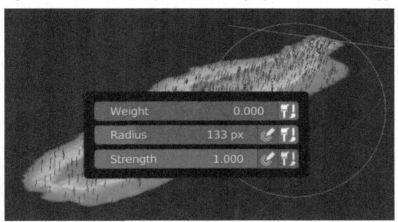

Figure 12.18 – Weight Paint brush options

Start painting the landscape edge we assigned earlier – try to make the heatmap you're creating as random as possible:

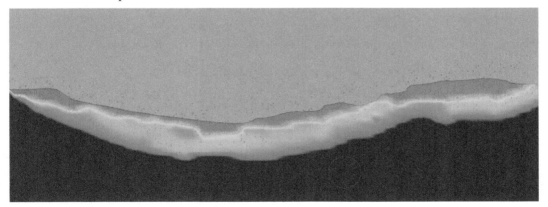

Figure 12.19 – Weight painting the landscape

This way, we'll be distributing the rocks and flowers in a random way, which is the natural way. Let's now replace the particles with the **Rock** object.

Replacing particles with the Rock object

The next step is to replace the **Hair** particles with the **Rock** object. To do that, go back to **Particle Properties**, scroll to the **Render** tab and switch **Render As** from **Path** to **Object**:

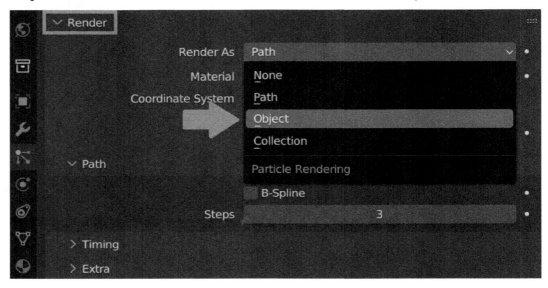

Figure 12.20 – Switching Render As to Object

Then, a new tab will show up called **Object**. Set **Instance Object** to the **Rock** object:

1. Set the **Scale** value of the object to 1.000 – by default, it's set to 0.050.
2. Increase **Scale Randomness** to 1.000:

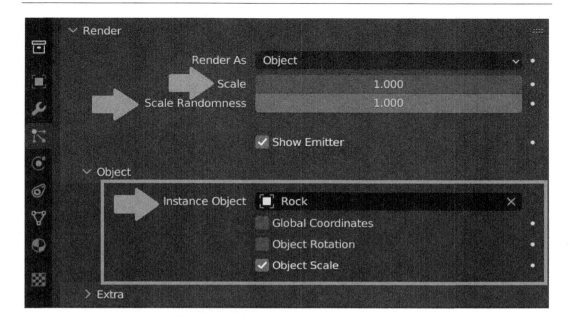

Figure 12.21 – Setting Instance Object to Rock

Now, we'll have the rocks scattered across the vertex group area we created:

Figure 12.22 – Scattering rocks in the landscape environment

The next step will be to randomize the rotation of the rocks. So far, they are all facing in the same direction. To change their rotation, go back to the **Particle Properties** settings and perform these steps:

1. Check the **Rotation** checkbox at the top.
2. Set **Orientation Axis** to **Global Z**.
3. Increase the **Randomize** value to 1.000:

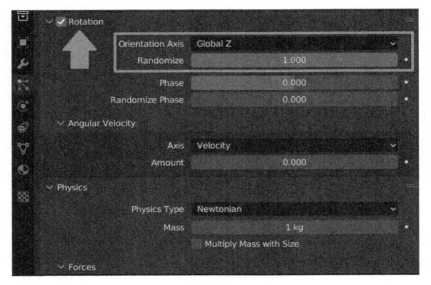

Figure 12.23 – Changing the Orientation Axis and Randomize values for Rock

This way, the rocks will be randomized, which makes them look natural.

Figure 12.24 – Randomizing the rocks' shape and scale in the landscape environment

You can control the number of rocks by changing the **Number** value under **Emission** as follows. I set it like so:

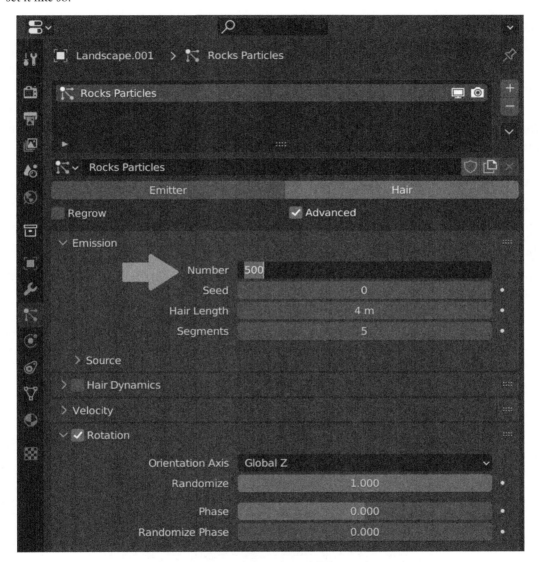

Figure 12.25 – Setting the number of rock particles to 500

Now, it's time to scatter flowers.

Scattering flowers in the landscape

Let's repeat the steps from the previous section to scatter flowers in the landscape – but here, the situation is different. We have multiple flower elements. Should we create a new particle system for every flower object? No, there is a better way. We'll be scattering the flowers as a collection.

You might wonder why we don't just put everything in a collection, the rocks and flowers, and use just one particle system. The answer is that rocks and flowers don't have the same characteristics. Rocks can be rotated on any axis, even flipped upside down, and they will remain rocks.

On the other hand, flowers don't share the same characteristics as rocks. Flowers can only rotate on the z axis. This is why we're putting flower objects inside a collection.

Putting flower objects inside a collection

Collections are a way Blender organizes scenes. Collections contain objects and everything else in a scene. You can use them to gather objects with the same characteristics: cars, or flowers in our case.

This makes the selection easier and keeps your scene organized.

You can create a collection in **Outline**, which is on the right-hand side of your Blender scene, by right-clicking and choosing **New Collection**:

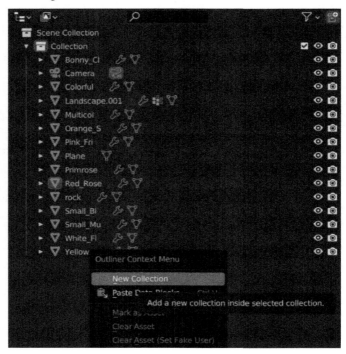

Figure 12.26 – Adding a new collection in Outline

Double-click on your collection and change its name to `Flowers`.

Next, drag all the flowers inside the **Flowers** collection by clicking on the orange triangles next to the flower objects.

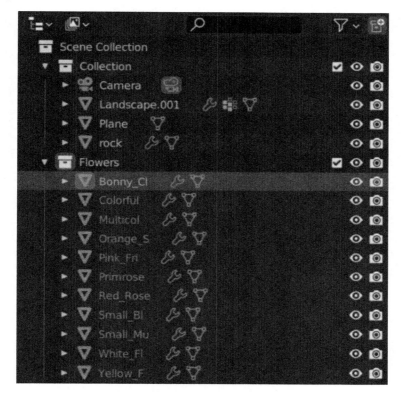

Figure 12.27 – Placing all the flowers in the Flowers collection

Now that we have the flowers inside a collection named **Flowers**, let's go back to our particle system.

The only change we'll be making is to the **Render** tab. The flowers are now a collection, not an object.

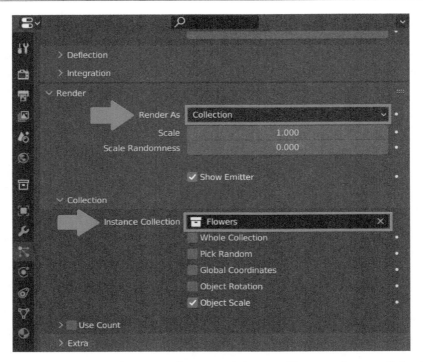

Figure 12.28 – Setting Render As to Collection and choosing Flowers as Instance Collection

This is how the flowers look when scattered in the landscape:

Figure 12.29 – Displaying rocks and flowers in the landscape environment

Still, we have some empty areas to fill. We need to find a way to duplicate the flowers without affecting the performance of our machine.

Boosting your Blender performance with one click

To make our scene look more natural, we have to increase the number of plant particles. But increasing the number of particles to the degree we want slows down the performance of our computer, which might cause Blender to freeze and crash. This is a pretty common problem when working with particle systems in Blender, but I have a fantastic solution for you, which is **Children** particles.

Based on the Blender 3.3 manual, **Children** particles originate from individual particles. They make it possible to work primarily with a relatively low number of **Parent** particles, from whom the physics are calculated.

To put it simply, **Children** particles make copies of existing particles to reduce the computational power needed without slowing down the performance.

To use the **Children** particles, go back to **Particle Properties**, and scroll down to **Children**:

1. Set the type to **Simple** under **Children**.
2. Increase both **Display Amount** and **Render Amount** to 5:

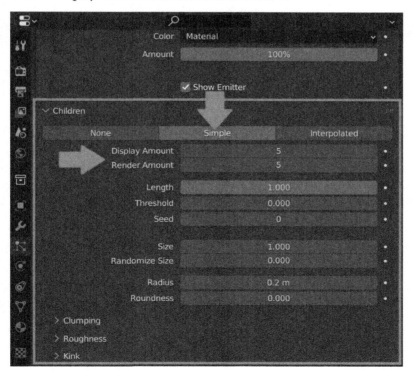

Figure 12.30 – Setting the type to Simple and Display Amount and Render Amount to 5

Now, we will have multiple duplications of our flower particles without affecting the performance of our machine.

To explain further, **Children** particles make copies of existing particles to reduce the computational power needed. They reuse the geometry data of the main flower particles.

Figure 12.31 – Final result of the scattered flowers and rocks in the landscape scene

There we go – our scene has all the essential elements to it!

Summary

To summarize this chapter. I can say that by adjusting the basic **Particle System** settings discussed here and experimenting with others, you can scatter any object you want in your environment while controlling the number, scale, and rotation of these objects.

In this chapter, we understood how to use **Particle System** in Blender to scatter flowers and rocks in our landscape environment. First, we learned what the **Particle System** option in Blender is and why you should use it.

In the next chapter, we will learn about rendering, setting up the camera, and compositing so that we can produce final realistic renders of our natural landscape 3D scene.

13

Finalizing the Landscape Scene – Lighting, Rendering, and Compositing

Now that you've created your landscape scene, you'll probably want to try rendering it. In this chapter, you'll learn how to aim your camera, render a scene, and apply some compositing tricks.

First, we will make some adjustments to the landscape shape, including improving the water material to make it better fit our landscape theme, and then set up some realistic lighting using an HDRI map and jump into rendering and compositing.

In this chapter, we'll be covering the following topics:

- Adjusting the landscape shape
- Improving the water material
- Setting realistic lighting in our scene
- Rendering our scene
- Compositing the scene

Technical requirements

This chapter requires a Mac or PC capable of running Blender Version 3.0 or above.

You can download the resources for this chapter from GitHub at `https://github.com/PacktPublishing/3D-Environment-Design-with-Blender/tree/main/chapter-13`

Adjusting the landscape shape

In order to have some excellent rendered images, it would be great if we could expand our landscape environment to fill in the empty areas in the background:

Figure 13.1 – Landscape scene with empty space in the background

To achieve this goal, let's create a new different landscape object (which we covered in *Chapter 6, Creating Realistic Landscapes in Blender*). Feel free to play with the landscape settings to achieve a different outcome.

One setting that should stay constant is the noise type. Set the new landscape noise type to **Slick Rock** so that it will be compatible with our first landscape.

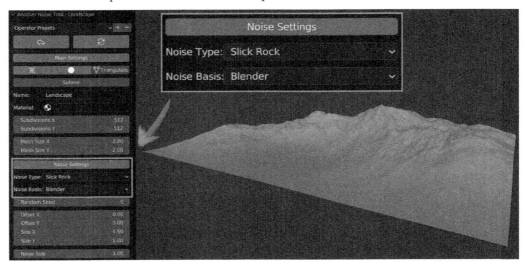

Figure 13.2 - Changing Noise Type to Slick Rock and Noise Basis to Blender

Next, move it forward and spin it around on the Z axis, like this:

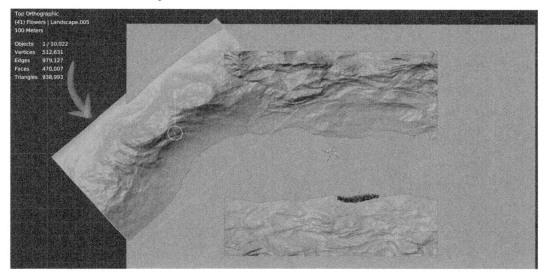

Figure 13.3 – Duplicating the landscape to fill in the empty space in the back

Now, we can see that our environment looks complete and pleasing to the eye.

Figure 13.4 – The landscape scene with more details in the back

Our new landscape doesn't have a material assigned, so let's texture it.

Assigning the mountain material to the new landscape

We need to assign the same mountain material assigned to the first landscape to the second one. To do that, let's follow these steps:

1. Select the new landscape.

2. Go to **Material Properties**, which you will find empty.

3. Click on the **Materials** library and choose the **Mountain** material.

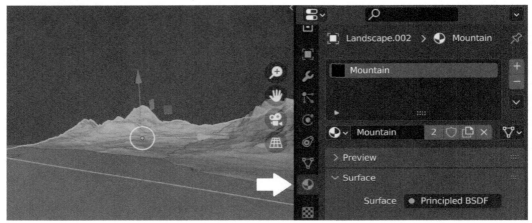

Figure 13.5 – Assigning the Mountain material to the second landscape

Now, our second landscape will look like the first one:

Figure 13.6 – Texturing the second landscape

This is the first change we apply to our landscape environment, and now the background of our landscape scene will be filled in and look more realistic. Next, let's tweak the water material.

Improving the water material

So far, the color of the water is bluish and doesn't look very realistic. The ground is muddy, and since the water is reflective, it should have a muddy color too, so we need to apply some tweaks to the water material.

Figure 13.7 – The landscape scene progress from Chapter 9

To tweak the water material, we first need to make a change to the **ColorRamp** node.

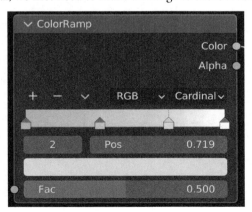

Figure 13.8 – Tweaking the ColorRamp node

Let's give the first three handles a creamy color that gradates from dark to light creamy. The last handle color is purely white.

The second change is to the **Mix** shader. Set the mix amount to 0.1 so that we can have only 10% of water transparency (in the **Transparent BSDF** node).

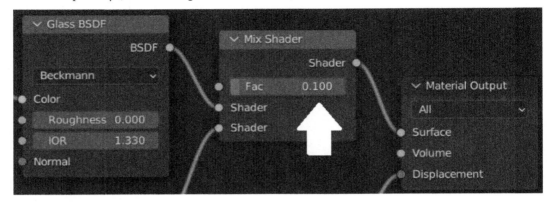

Figure 13.9 – Reducing the Mix shader Fac value to 0.1

Here's the full node setup of the water material:

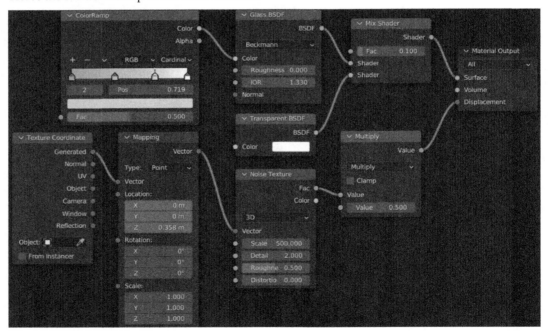

Figure 13.10 – The new node setup of the water material

The water with the changes applied now looks like this in **Rendered Preview** mode:

Figure 13.11 – Rendering the new water material

The water blended better with the muddy color of the landscape and now looks more realistic than before.

Now, let's set up realistic lighting in our scene by using HDRI maps.

Setting realistic lighting in our scene

To set up realistic lighting in our scene, we'll be using an HDRI map. HDRI maps are one of the most efficient and quickest ways to light a 3D scene and achieve realistic results in Blender. HDRI maps are typically 360-degree panoramic images of real-world lighting containing accurate lighting detail.

Let's get started on using an HDRI map in our scene. The one shown in *Figure 13.12* is what we'll be using; it has a nice sun reflection. We can use it to emit light into our landscape scene to achieve accurate lighting, resulting in more realistic 3D renders.

Figure 13.12 – An HDRI map used to lighten the scene

You can download the HDRI map using this link: https://github.com/PacktPublishing/3D-Environment-Design-with-Blender/blob/a15652a3e7b406a7c70cd8b63837922aea6b151b/chapter-13/HDRI.zip.

You can refer to the *Using a Blender Sky Texture node to light our environment* section in *Chapter 5, Achieve Photorealistic Lighting in Your Environment with Blender*, to learn how to assign and tweak HDRI maps in Blender.

With the lighting set, our next move is to start rendering our landscape scene.

Rendering our scene

One of the most important aspects to learn when becoming a 3D artist is how to create professional-looking renders of the scenes you created. However, before giving your scene a render, you need to add a camera to your scene and put it in a specific viewport.

Adding a camera to a scene

Adding a camera to your scene is simple. Press *Shift + A* in the 3D Viewport, scroll down, and you will find the **Camera** object. When you add the **Camera** object, it will appear in your scene, as shown here:

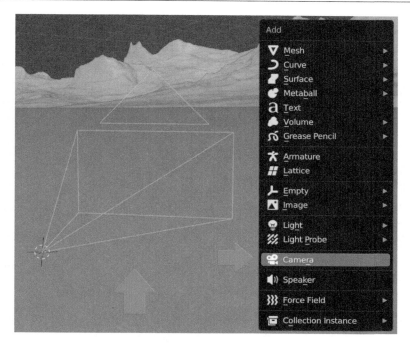

Figure 13.13 – Adding a Camera object to a scene

Next, we need to correctly position our camera for rendering. So, let's find the best shot by navigating to a point in our 3D Viewport that includes everything – the landscape, water, flowers, and rocks – as shown here:

Figure 13.14 – Picking the best shot to position the camera

Now, we want the camera to be pointing at this scene. To put it in this position, we need to press *Ctrl + Alt + 0.*

You'll be pointing the camera at your current view. You will see the following frame:

Figure 13.15 – Pointing the camera at the current view

What's inside the frame is what's going to be included in the rendered image.

If you want to exit the camera view or return to it, you can press the *0* hotkey on the numpad.

Before rendering our scene, let's tweak the rendering settings in the **Render Properties** tab.

Changing the rendering engine

In order to achieve maximum realism, we need to use the **Cycles** render engine. Let's switch first to **Render Properties** and set the render engine to **Cycles**.

Please refer to the *Differences between the three render engines of Blender* section in *Chapter 5, Achieve Photorealistic Lighting in Your Environment with Blender*, to understand the difference between the rendering engines in Blender.

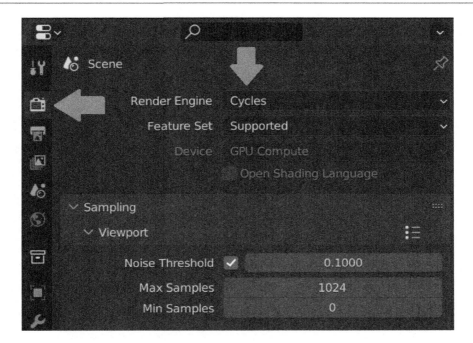

Figure 13.16 – Switching the render engine to Cycles

Next, let's tweak the next rendering setting, which is the number of samples.

What is the right number of samples to use?

Samples are the number of paths to trace for each pixel in the final render. As more samples are taken, the final render becomes less noisy and more accurate but takes longer to complete.

Blender gives us three ways to control rendering samples:

- By setting **Max Samples**, Blender will stop the rendering process once that number of samples is reached.
- For **Min Samples**, Blender should always exceed the **Min Samples** value when rendering.
- For **Time Limit**, you can set a timer – for example, 5 minutes. This means that Blender will keep rendering the image until a time limit of 5 minutes is reached. The number of samples rendered will be based on how powerful your setup is. Faster computers will render with more samples.

The more samples you use, the clearer your rendered image will be, but it will also take longer to be rendered.

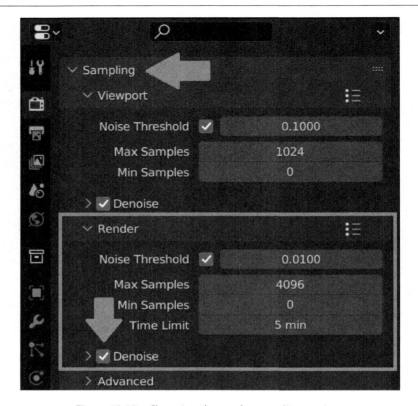

Figure 13.17 – Changing the render sampling settings

In our case, let's set the **Time Limit** value under the **Render** tab to 5 minutes. A time limit is a more precise way to control the render time, especially when rendering large animations. A 30-second, 24-frames-per-second animation rendered at 5 minutes per render will render for exactly 60 hours (30 x 24 x 5 = 3,600 minutes = 60 hours).

Also, make sure that the **Denoise** box is checked so that we can have a clear final render without noise. However, keep in mind that with too few samples, denoising won't work properly and can lead to a loss of details in some areas of your render.

Changing the rendered image resolution

You can control the render image size – for example, the default settings are 1,920 px on the X axis and 1,080 px on the Y axis, meaning that this is a 2K image quality render. You can change it to 4K by increasing the 100% value to 200%, or decrease it to 50% for 1K quality.

Keep in mind that when increasing the render image scale to 200%, the render time will quadruple, as the number of pixels is squared. This means that if it takes 5 minutes to render a 1,920 x 1,080 image, it will take 20 minutes to render a 4K image.

Figure 13.18 – The difference between 2K and 4K resolution

To change the resolution of your render, go to the **Output** properties, and under the **Format** tab, you will find **Resolution X** and **Y**, and the percentage set at **100%**.

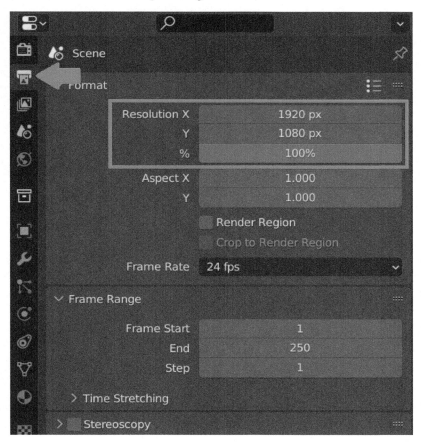

Figure 13.19 – Changing the rendered image resolution

Rendering the landscape scene

Let's go ahead and give our scene a render by going to the **Render** tab on the top bar. You can access **Render Image** by using the *F12* hotkey.

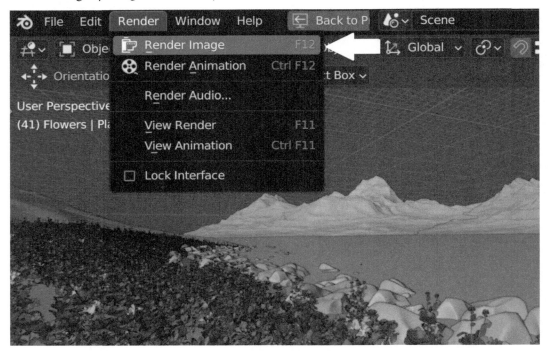

Figure 13.20 – Rendering the scene from the camera view

Immediately, a new window will pop up, showing your render getting clearer and clearer until it is finished.

Upon completion, go to **Image** and click on **Save As…**. Locate the destination where you want to save your image. This way, you'll be saving the render as an image on your computer.

Figure 13.21 – Saving the rendered image

The following figure shows our saved rendered image:

Figure 13.22 – The saved rendered image of our project

Now that we have our scene rendered, the next step is to work on compositing to make it stand out.

Compositing the scene

Compositing allows us to add awesome effects to our final render to make it look more believable. We can change the mood of our render, giving it a cold, bluish look or a warm, sunny feeling.

To switch to compositing, you need to make sure that you have already rendered your scene; otherwise, there will be no initial input to work with under the **Compositing** tab.

At the top of your Blender scene, you'll find a bunch of tabs. Go to **Compositing** and check the **Use Nodes** box.

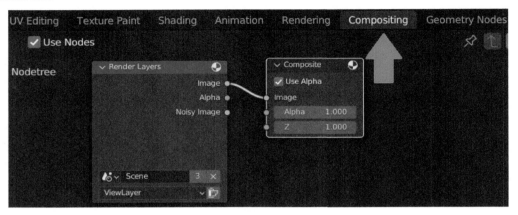

Figure 13.23 – Switching to the Compositing tab in Blender

To see our render in the background, let's press *Shift + A* and search for the **Viewer** node:

Connect the **Render Layers Image** slot to the **Image** slot of the **Viewer** node. This way, we'll be able to see the render displayed in the background.

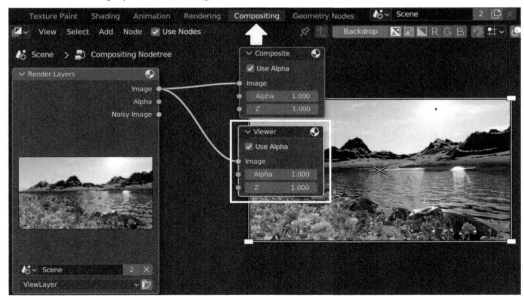

Figure 13.24 – Adding the Viewer node in our compositing setup

Let's start with the first compositing effect, which is color balance.

Using the Color Balance node

The **Color Balance** node adjusts the color and values of our render, and we can give our final render a different feeling based on the color we choose.

Press *Shift + A* and add a **Color Balance** node.

Place it between the **Render Layers** node and the **Composite** and **Viewer** nodes.

Figure 13.25 – Adding the Color Balance node in our compositing setup

Now, in the **Color Balance** node, let's change the color of the last circle, **Gain**, to blue. This way, we'll have a blue, cold feeling in our scene.

Figure 13.26 – Changing the overall color of our render to bluish

On the other hand, if we change the color of the **Color Balance** node to red, we'll give our scene a warm feeling.

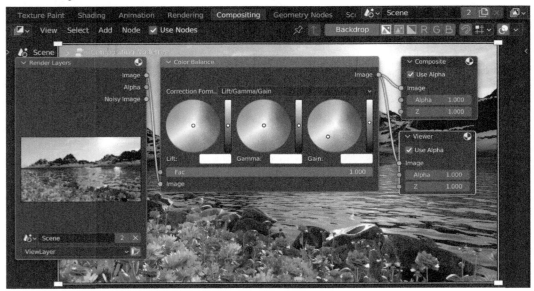

Figure 13.27 – Giving our render a warm feeling

Let's add a second compositing effect to our render, which is **Glare**.

Adding Glare to the render

The **Glare** node is used to add lens flares for glows around exposed parts, such as the sun or bright lights of an image.

To add the **Glare** node, press *Shift + A*:

1. Put the node in between the **Render Layers** and **Color Balance** nodes.

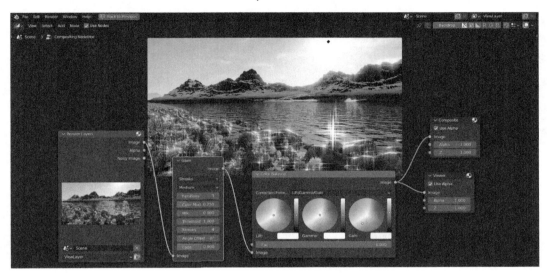

Figure 13.28 – The Glare compositing node set to Streaks

Immediately, you will see the nice stars on your render. In our case, we want to use a glow.

2. Change the **Glare** type from **Streaks** to **Fog Glow**.

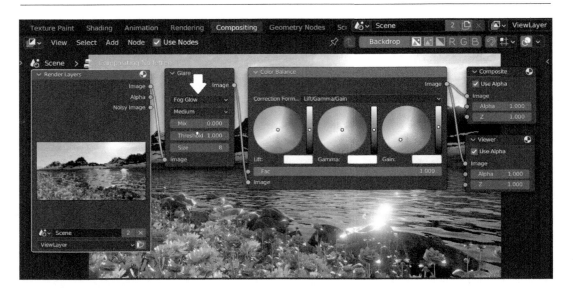

Figure 13.29 – The Glare compositing node set to Fog Glow

3. You can control the amount of glare by increasing the **Size** value to 8 or 9, depending on the brightness you want to have in your render.

Figure 13.30 – Applying the Glare node to the rendered image in the compositing setup

And there you have it – the final result of our landscape environment render.

Summary

Thank you for reading this book through to the end; I hope it gave you the information you were looking for to create photorealistic 3D environments in Blender.

In this last chapter, we achieved the final goal of this book, which is to make realistic landscape renders in Blender.

We started by applying some final adjustments to the water material and to the landscape shape to make it look more pleasing to the eye when rendered.

We also learned how to add cameras to our scene and how to place them in the right place to capture a good view of the landscape scene. Then, we learned how to render our scene and save the rendered image.

Then, we applied some compositing tricks to our render, such as glare and color balance, to affect the mood of our render and make it stand out.

We did it – we started from nothing and went all the way to the end to create this nice, realistic landscape render. How amazing is that?

You might not be able to achieve good, realistic results on your first attempt, and that's completely fine. You should not be discouraged by that. My advice to you is repetition. Photorealism is a skill, and every skill requires repetition to be mastered.

Recreate the landscape scene, tweak it, play with the settings differently, and try new things. This will give you a greater understanding of how Blender works in general.

Of course, your journey through the world of 3D photorealism has only just begun, and you will build many more incredible projects along the way. And maybe, one day, your creations will be seen by people worldwide.

Thank you for sticking with me all the way to the end of this book.

Your friend, Abdelilah Hamdani.

Peace.

Index

www.packtpub.com

Subscribe to our online digital library for full access to over 7,000 books and videos, as well as industry leading tools to help you plan your personal development and advance your career. For more information, please visit our website.

Why subscribe?

- Spend less time learning and more time coding with practical eBooks and Videos from over 4,000 industry professionals
- Improve your learning with Skill Plans built especially for you
- Get a free eBook or video every month
- Fully searchable for easy access to vital information
- Copy and paste, print, and bookmark content

Did you know that Packt offers eBook versions of every book published, with PDF and ePub files available? You can upgrade to the eBook version at packtpub.com and as a print book customer, you are entitled to a discount on the eBook copy. Get in touch with us at customercare@packtpub.com for more details.

At www.packtpub.com, you can also read a collection of free technical articles, sign up for a range of free newsletters, and receive exclusive discounts and offers on Packt books and eBooks.

Other Books You May Enjoy

If you enjoyed this book, you may be interested in these other books by Packt:

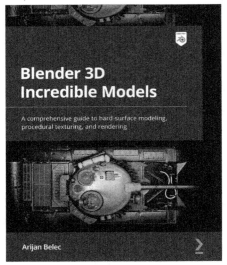

Blender 3D Incredible Models

Arijan Belec

ISBN: 978-1-80181-781-3

- Dive into the fundamental theory behind hard-surface modeling
- Explore Blender's extensive modeling tools and features
- Use references to produce sophisticated and accurate models
- Create models with realistic textures and materials
- Set up lighting and render your scenes with style
- Master the use of polygons to make game-optimized models
- Develop impressive animations by exploring the world of rigging
- Employ texture painting and modifiers to render the tiniest details

Blender 3D By Example - Second Edition

Oscar Baechler , Xury Greer

ISBN: 978-1-78961-256-1

- Explore core 3D modeling tools in Blender such as extrude, bevel, and loop cut
- Understand Blender's Outliner hierarchy, collections, and modifiers
- Find solutions to common problems in modeling 3D characters and designs
- Implement lighting and probes to liven up an architectural scene using EEVEE
- Produce a final rendered image complete with lighting and post-processing effects
- Learn character concept art workflows and how to use the basics of Grease Pencil
- Learn how to use Blender's built-in texture painting tools

Packt is searching for authors like you

If you're interested in becoming an author for Packt, please visit `authors.packtpub.com` and apply today. We have worked with thousands of developers and tech professionals, just like you, to help them share their insight with the global tech community. You can make a general application, apply for a specific hot topic that we are recruiting an author for, or submit your own idea.

Hi!

I am Abdelilah Hamdani, author of *3D Environment Design with Blender,* really hope you enjoyed reading this book and found it useful for increasing your productivity and efficiency in 3D photorealistic environment design and Blender in general.

It would really help us (and other potential readers!) if you could leave a review on Amazon sharing your final 3d environment landscape result.

Go to the link below or scan the QR code to leave your review:

`https://packt.link/r/1803235853`

Your review will help us to understand what's worked well in this book, and what could be improved upon for future editions, so it really is appreciated.

Best wishes,

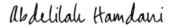

Download a free PDF copy of this book

Thanks for purchasing this book!

Do you like to read on the go but are unable to carry your print books everywhere?

Is your eBook purchase not compatible with the device of your choice?

Don't worry, now with every Packt book you get a DRM-free PDF version of that book at no cost.

Read anywhere, any place, on any device. Search, copy, and paste code from your favorite technical books directly into your application.

The perks don't stop there, you can get exclusive access to discounts, newsletters, and great free content in your inbox daily

Follow these simple steps to get the benefits:

1. Scan the QR code or visit the link below

https://packt.link/free-ebook/9781803235851

2. Submit your proof of purchase
3. That's it! We'll send your free PDF and other benefits to your email directly

Printed in Great Britain
by Amazon

34782758R00192